MEET NORTH AFRICA

A Berber village boy of Morocco stands beneath a great fortress high up
in the Atlas Mountains

MEET

NORTH AFRICA

────────

BY

JOHN GUNTHER

WITH SAM AND BERYL EPSTEIN

HAMISH HAMILTON
LONDON

First published in Great Britain, 1958
by Hamish Hamilton Ltd
90 Great Russell Street, London, W.C.1
Copyright © 1958 by John Gunther,
Samuel Epstein and Beryl Williams Epstein

Part of the material in this book first appeared in Inside
Africa. *Copyright © 1953, 1954, 1955 by John Gunther*

MADE IN GREAT BRITAIN AT THE PITMAN PRESS, BATH

CONTENTS

ILLUSTRATIONS

*All the illustrations are reproduced by kind permission of
Hulton Picture Library*

The map facing page 1 was drawn by Pamela Fowler

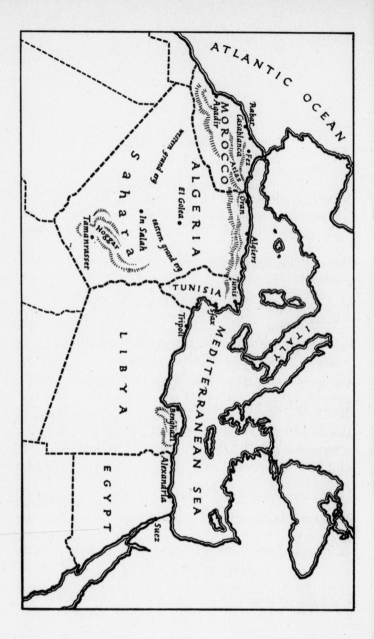

1

The Land—and a Bit of History

THIS is an interesting time to meet North Africa. Most people in this romantic region have just won—or are still struggling to win—their independence from foreign rulers. Here the very old and the very new are living side by side—or, in some cases, coming together in a head-on collision. When I visited North Africa recently I travelled in a few hours, by plane, across hundreds of miles of the world's greatest desert, the vast and mysterious Sahara. But below me, as I flew above the rocky and sandy wastes, I could see a long line of camels following a caravan route centuries old.

The high ranges of the Atlas Mountains, rising between the desert and the Mediterranean coast, are now dotted here and there with hydroelectric stations and up-to-date mining enterprises. But the shepherds who tend their flocks of goats and sheep in those mountains still wear the same long hooded cloaks their ancestors wore, and still live in much the same primitive way that their people have lived for hundreds of years.

It can be very cold in those mountains, incidentally—a fact which surprises many who take for granted that all of North Africa is warm. During a recent winter many hill villages were completely snowed in, and had to receive supplies by parachute. And even along the coastal slope of those mountains, the earth turns to frozen mud in the winter months. Of course North Africa can be hot, fiercely hot, at times. In the desert areas the thermometer may remain far above the hundred-degree mark every day for weeks on end in the summer. But even the Sahara can be bitterly cold as soon as the sun goes down at night.

A wise Frenchman once said the land was "a cold country with a hot sun," and that is probably as good a way to describe it as any.

The North Africa you will meet in this book consists of four countries: Morocco, Algeria, Tunisia and Libya.

We might include two other countries as well—Egypt and the Spanish Sahara. But there isn't much to be said about the arid, sparsely settled strip of coastland called the Spanish Sahara. And Egypt is really a part of the Middle East—an area including Syria, Israel, Saudi Arabia and other Asian lands beyond the Suez Canal and the Red Sea. Egypt's history has sometimes been closely tied up with the history of the rest of North Africa, but on the whole she is more of a Middle Eastern than an African country.

Morocco, Algeria, Tunisia and Libya, on the other hand, have often been closely involved with Europe. They are situated right across one of the

greatest of Old World thoroughfares, the Mediterranean. For thousands of years settlers, soldiers and
traders, sailing back and forth across that sea, have
kept North Africa bound to the lands on its opposite
shore. Men have always crossed the Mediterranean
more easily, in fact, than the massive "sea of sand"
at North Africa's back. This explains why North
Africa has never had much to do with the part of
the continent below the Sahara. It also explains why
some North African cities, and even North African
grain fields and olive groves, look so much like cities,
fields and groves in Italy or Spain.

The earliest known settlers of North Africa probably came from Europe more than three thousand
years ago, long before the boundaries of our present
four North African countries existed. Those settlers
were primitive farmers called Berbers—white-
skinned people, some of them very fair, with blue
eyes—whose descendants make up one of the largest
and most important groups of people inhabiting
North Africa today.

The name "Berber" comes from the old Latin
word, *barbari*, or "foreigners"—the same word that
gives us "barbarian." This is not the name they use
for themselves. They call themselves Imazighen,
which in their own language means "free men."
But they have not always been free, because their
countries have been invaded over and over again—
by Phoenicians, Romans, Vandals, Arabs, Turks
and the modern European armies of France, Spain
and Italy. All these strangers from other parts of the
Mediterranean world, fighting and conquering in
North Africa, have soaked this land with their blood

and the blood of the Berbers. And all of them have left their marks on this huge stretch of mountain and desert.

A GLIMPSE BACKWARD

The first of these invaders, the Phoenicians, came to North Africa in about 1200 B.C. In what is now Tunisia, they built the magnificent city of Carthage, and they ruled the whole Mediterranean from this great metropolis where 700,000 people are said to have lived. The Carthaginians grew rich on trade, and on the valuable purplish-red dye they made from tiny snails found along the North African coast. They built houses seven stories tall, and had a powerful army that used elephants in much the same way that a modern army uses tanks. One stable in Carthage housed three hundred of the big ivory-tusked beasts which could be captured in those days in North African forests.

For almost a thousand years Carthage had things pretty much her own way in most of North Africa and all around the western edge of the Mediterranean. Then the city of Rome rose up on the opposite shore of the Mediterranean, and the Romans made up their minds to conquer the Punics, as they called the Carthaginians.

Three wars fought between Rome and Carthage, known as the Punic Wars, began in 245 B.C. and didn't end until ninety-nine years later, when Roman soldiers burned Carthage to the ground.

The great fire blazed for ten long days, while hundreds of terrified Carthaginians hurled themselves from the roofs of their tall houses in frantic efforts to escape the flames. When the fire was over at last, the power of Carthage was destroyed and Carthage itself was a heap of blackened rubble.

For the next six hundred years North Africa was a part of the great Roman Empire, and was ruled by governors sent from Rome. From North Africa's forests Rome took lions and other wild beasts to exhibit in her circuses. From North African farms she took crowded shiploads of grain, olive oil, wine and wool. But Rome gave the land fine new cities, with roads to bind them together and aqueducts to supply them with water from the hills. In fact, the Romans built so sturdily that many of their buildings and roads and aqueducts are still in existence there today.

Next came the Vandals; these blond giants from Central Europe ousted Rome from North Africa in the year 439 and held the land themselves for a century. They did little building of their own, and used the well-built Roman roads and towns. They were barbarians, and have left few traces for us to see.

The next great invasion into North Africa changed it for all time to come. This was made by bronzed, powerful Arabs from east of the Red Sea, and they totally remade the face of North Africa.

The first of these conquering Arabs belonged to separate pagan tribes, as the Berbers did. But a prophet rose among them, by name Mohammed, who united them within a few short, vivid years under his leadership and the banner of the god he called Allah. In Allah's name they determined to conquer the world. And in a vast campaign, which lasted over a century, they did conquer Egypt, all of North Africa and the whole southern half of Europe.

But North Africa, with its sturdy and stubborn people, gave the Arabs a lot of trouble. In fact, the Berbers fought the Arabs tooth and nail. To this day people in North Africa tell stories about a woman named the Cahena, who led them in some of their battles, and about the struggle between the Berbers and one famous Arab commander, Sidi Okba. While that struggle lasted, the stories say, "blood flowed across the earth like the waves of the sea."

Sidi Okba (*Sidi* is an Arabic word that means something like "His Excellency") won most of his earlier battles, and when each engagement was over he cut off a finger or an ear of the vanquished leader.

"That is to teach you a lesson," he said. "Now you will always remember the Arabs." And after this unpleasant ceremony Sidi Okba always rode off in search of further triumphs. But he didn't install a governor over his defeated enemies, as the Romans had done, or leave an army behind to control them. So as soon as he left each place, the surviving Berbers began to prepare themselves for the time when they could fight him again.

Sidi Okba drove his men straight across North Africa, clear to the Atlantic. There, legend says, he rode his horse into the breakers, and shouted his anger at the sea for putting an end to his conquests. But when Sidi Okba turned back from the sea, the Berbers were waiting for him. And, as he rode eastward, they defeated him over and over again, and finally killed him.

Still the Arabs hadn't given up their resolution to take North Africa. New armies—a second wave—surged westward out of Egypt, mounted on horses or on the shambling camels which frightened the Berbers because they had never seen camel-riding soldiers before. And at last, in about the year 700, the Arabs felt they had made North Africa a permanent part of the vast empire they were building in Allah's name, the empire they called Islam.

True, most Berbers by this time believed in Allah too, and had become Mohammedans—or, as it is more correct to say, Moslems. Accepting a new religion was not difficult for them. In the past they had adopted, in turn, the pagan gods of Carthage and of Rome, and the one God worshipped by the small groups of Jews who had come into North Africa from time to time. Some Berbers also turned Christian. One young Berber, son of a pagan father, became so important in the Christian Church that he is still revered by Christians everywhere as St. Augustine.

It was also true that some Berbers—partly for the glory of Allah, partly for the booty they hoped to win—joined willingly in the next great Arab campaign, the one against Spain. A Berber warrior named Tarik fought so successfully in that country that a huge rocky mount on the Spanish coast was named in his honour. Its name, *Jebel Tarik*, or Hill of Tarik, has come down to us over the years as Gibraltar.

But even after the Berbers had helped the Arabs

win brilliant new victories, it was clear that the
Arabs and Berbers didn't really like or trust each
other. In fact the Arabs soon realized that they had
been much mistaken when they thought of North
Africa as safely in their hands. The governors they sent
to rule the land had a very difficult time.

In some cases the Berbers hated an Arab governor,
and rebelled against him, simply because he was a
foreigner. But in other cases they hated him because
they thought he wasn't a good Moslem. Only by understanding what had happened after Mohammed's
death can we see that this wasn't quite as strange as
it may sound.

And now a word about the Prophet Mohammed.
He was more than merely a religious leader. He led
his people into battle and ruled them. When he died
his empire had no leader. He had no sons of his own,
and he had named no heir. So his followers, arguing
about what to do, divided sharply into two groups.

One group said that their new leader might be
anyone they cared to elect by the same system they
normally used to name leaders for their tribes.
Members of this group called themselves Sunnites.
The other group wanted some member of Mohammed's family to lead them, so that they could call
him Mohammed's true caliph, a title that means
"successor." Their candidate was a man named Ali,
who was Mohammed's nephew and married to
Mohammed's daughter, Fatima. After Ali's death,
this group wanted to set up a royal family, descended
from Mohammed, which would rule all Moslems
for ever. These people came to be called Shiites,
from the Arabic word *shi'a* which means "party."

The arguments between Sunnites and Shiites split up the Moslem empire during Ali's own lifetime, and it has never been united under a single leader since then. Even now the two groups have different ideas, just as Protestants and Catholics have different ideas even though both groups are Christian.

Of course the Berbers took part in these arguments too, and the arguments often developed into bloody wars that sometimes brought glory and sometimes misery to their land.

An Arab named Idris, for example, one of Ali's many descendants, became an enemy of the Shiite caliph because the caliph belonged to another sect. So Idris escaped into North Africa, captured the loyalty of several Berber tribes and set up his own kingdom in what is now Morocco.

Finally the Caliph Harun-al-Rashid—the same caliph who appears in that famous book, *A Thousand and One Nights*—grew tired of trying to defeat the several new kingdoms that were springing up in North Africa. Before his death, in about the year 800, he gave up his claim to the whole territory. Some Arab leaders remained in North Africa, but only because they had the support of Berber followers. Others fled hastily back to the Arab capital, then in Baghdad.

THE GOLDEN AGE

Now, for the first time since the Phoenician invasion two thousand years earlier, North Africa was ruled by its own people, free of foreign ties. And now North Africa, in the hands of North Africans, entered into the glorious period of her history which is sometimes called her Golden Age. At the very moment when Europe was sinking into the centuries of poverty and ignorance known as the Dark Ages, North Africa on the other side of the Mediterranean was beginning to blaze and swell with triumph.

Three kinds of men made the land rich and strong: soldiers, traders and scholars.

The soldiers, who were called Saracens by their enemies, earned an unmatched reputation for cruelty. In those days the head of a North African kingdom thought nothing of killing his sons and younger brothers if he believed they might some day threaten his power. One ruler, it was said, sat calmly on his throne while he stabbed to the heart five hundred enemies as they were brought before him one by one. But the North African soldiers were brave as well as cruel. They marched again into Spain, as they had done before. They seized the island of Sicily in the centre of the Mediterranean. They even invaded Italy.

The traders were equally successful in their own way. Their camel caravans, a method of trade they had learned from the Arabs, travelled hundreds of miles to the south and to the east. Some brought back treasure from beyond the Sahara, others from ports served by ships sailing the Indian Ocean and the Red Sea. Spices, silks, perfumes, gold, precious stones, ivory and ostrich plumes flowed into North Africa in a brilliant and sumptuous stream.

To all this new wealth, partly earned by trade,

partly won in battle, were also added huge sums collected in taxes from all non-Moslems—that is, from Christians and Jews. The land became rich beyond the dreams of any ordinary men. It acquired new cities. The domes of its mosques glowed with gold and sparkled with jewel-coloured tiles. Rare plants blossomed in its gardens, and its fountains spouted water that in some cases had to be brought for miles across the desert.

Looking back from our own time we know that the empires the North African soldiers built didn't last for ever, and that the wealth of those empires didn't long outlast their power. But the third group of men who helped to create North Africa's Golden Age—the scholars who taught and studied at the many new universities built at that time—were amassing a kind of treasure that has survived until our own day.

The treasure they collected was knowledge, the knowledge on which much of modern science, art and industry are built.

Part of what those scholars collected was as old as the ancient Greeks, or older. The Romans learned what the Greeks knew, and made tremendous use of it in their own civilization. But by this time their knowledge had been largely forgotten all over Europe. It might have been forgotten everywhere for ever, if North Africa's scholars, and others like them in the Arab lands to the east, hadn't translated and preserved the classical Greek writings. To the knowledge in those writings they added new ideas of their own and ideas picked up in far countries like Persia, India and China.

These scholars wrote in Arabic, the language that was slowly becoming the language of most of North Africa—although many Berbers went on speaking their own tongues and still speak them now.

Our words *sloop*, *cable*, *traffic* and *tariff* all come from Arabic, and remind us that the Arabs had a wide knowledge of sailing, navigation and commerce.

Our word *algebra* comes from Arabic and so does *zero*, to remind us that the Arabs knew a great deal about the science of mathematics. And the numbers we use today are what we rightly call Arabic numerals.

Our words *lemon*, *rice* and *sugar*, all from Arabic, tell us that the Arabs knew a good deal about farming and agriculture.

Betelgeuse, the Arabic name we use for one of the stars, reminds us that Arabs knew a great deal about astronomy.

These scholars took great pride in their expert translations of Greek and Latin works into Arabic. And, like all other Arab-speaking people, they also loved the language for its own sake, as an instrument of sheer pleasure and delight. Graceful Arabic letters, carved or painted on a wall or a panel, were used as decorations on hundreds of buildings in North Africa. The recitation of long poems or stories in Arabic always drew—and still does today—eager crowds of listeners. Since the days of those scholars, in fact, the Arabic language, written and spoken by men who love it, has given a special grace and flavour to the whole land of North Africa.

A TIME OF TROUBLES

For a good many years those newly independent North African kingdoms, all rich and powerful, fought only when they crossed the Mediterranean to add to their European empires or to defend them. On their own soil they lived fairly peaceably together. When fighting did begin again it was mostly caused by rivalries between the various Moslem sects, each of which wanted religious as well as temporal power.

Early in the tenth century, for example, a group of Berber tribes who called themselves the Fatimites, after Mohammed's daughter Fatima, set out to conquer Egypt. In that distant eastern land, on the Nile, they built the new city of Cairo. And when the Fatimite leader decided to make Cairo his headquarters, he chose a young Berber soldier to serve as a sort of subking over North Africa.

Later came fierce warfare, when the Berbers and others in the North African hinterland refused to obey the Fatimite kings in Egypt. The Fatimites, to punish the North Africans, offered all of North Africa as a gift to certain wild Arab tribes. So began the second Arab invasion of North Africa.

Whole tribes of Arabs rode westward, plundering as they went. They were like a devouring cloud of locusts.

They burned towns. They captured herds of sheep, killed enough for a riotous feast and slaughtered the rest for sport. They pastured their horses in fields of ripe grain. They destroyed irrigation systems that had operated for centuries. They tore out grapevines, stripped olive and fig trees bare and then chopped up the trunks for firewood. Earth that had been green and fruitful and lovely became a barren waste under their ravaging hands.

These Arab invaders were nomads—roving herdsmen who cared nothing for agriculture or irrigation. They did, however, understand the value of North Africa's trade, and under their canny management the exchange of goods with foreigners grew more and more lucrative.

Meantime, across the Mediterranean, Europe was slowly rousing herself out of the Dark Ages. Her awakening—her Renaissance, as it is usually called —came about largely because she had begun to borrow some of the knowledge the Arab scholars were preserving. With this awakening new European kingdoms began to rise and grow wealthy. At first they willingly paid for the silks, gold, rare jewels and rarer spices that only North African traders could supply. But finally they grew jealous of North Africa's trade monopoly, and decided to use some of their newly borrowed knowledge to seek out trade routes of their own, so that they could deal directly with India, China, the Spice Islands and the lands below the Sahara.

And so it happened that European sailors, often following maps Arabic scholars had drawn, made the daring voyages that changed the face of this globe. They sailed around the Cape of Good Hope and across the Indian Ocean. One of them, a man named Christopher Columbus, who was seeking a westward passage to India, found instead a whole New World.

Almost overnight, it seemed, North Africa, already devastated by the Arabs, lost her position as middleman, or agent, for the bulk of the world's trade. And with it she lost what was left of her power and wealth.

The years that followed were grim years for North Africa. Even as early as 1492 her soldiers were driven out of Spain where they had lorded it over a European population for seven centuries. They lost Sicily. The Christian invaders from Sicily attacked them. And the Christian invasion from Sicily was only one of the long series of Crusades which Europeans were by then waging against the "infidels," as they sneeringly called all Moslems.

Suddenly then, Turkey, swollen with conquests all around the eastern end of the Mediterranean, decided to add North Africa to her empire. Most of Europe, busy building colonies across the Atlantic, showed little interest, and the North African kingdoms—except mountain-protected Morocco—were too weak to help themselves. Turkey's victory was swift and easy. Quickly she set up governors, called by the title of dey or bey, in each North African province east of Morocco.

ENTER THE PIRATES—ALSO THE UNITED STATES

So most of North Africa once more lost its independence, and came again under the rule of foreign overlords. But these newly arrived Turks were actually less hated than they might have been. For one thing they were Moslems. The ruler of Turkey used the title of Sultan, just as the ruler of Morocco did, and claimed to be a descendant of Mohammed. This meant that the Turks, too, were enemies of the Christians, whom the North Africans hated. And, for another thing, the Turkish governors enthusiastically encouraged the new breed of men who were beginning to thrive along the North African coast. These were men who lived by piracy, and who came to be known as the Barbary corsairs.

The North African pirates were not ashamed of growing rich on this illegal form of trade, now that their countries no longer controlled most of the world's legal commerce. Besides, since to them all Christians were enemies, they looked on Christian ships as fair game, to be seized in Allah's name. Piracy to them, in other words, was partly a religious duty and partly a profitable business. They organized it on a businesslike basis and carried it out with fanatical zeal.

The model for all the new pirate communities along the coast was the city of Algiers, which had become a pirate stronghold even before Turkey claimed it. That's where the red-bearded Barbarossa brothers established themselves, to become perhaps the most famous pirates of all time. The stories told about them fairly drip with gore, but they fought in Allah's name.

By the beginning of the seventeenth century Tunis and Tripoli, like Algiers, were living luxuriously on pirate earnings. The city of Salé in independent Morocco had its pirates too—the rest of the world called them "Sally Rovers"—and Salé became rich on booty seized at sea.

The Barbary pirates captured cargoes of all kinds. Also they took as prisoners the unfortunate passengers and crews, who were Christians as often as not. They made the strongest of the prisoners work as galley slaves. The rest were put up for sale at auctions that attracted wealthy buyers from all over the Moslem world.

The Christian world protested loudly, of course, at the thought of Christian men, women and children being sold into slavery. The Moslems ignored the protests. They knew that Christians were buying and selling slaves themselves at that very time. There was just one difference between the two trades, and to the Moslems it seemed small. The Christians dealt in pagan Negro slaves seized from their homes south of the Sahara, and in Moslem slaves when they could get them. The Moslems preferred slaves that were white-skinned and of Christian faith.

Today, with slavery outlawed practically all over the world, we can see that the slave-owning Christians didn't have a very strong moral case against the Moslems.

But the European powers did not act in unison to stamp out piracy. Each nation played for itself, hoping that its own ships would be let alone. England, for example, sent word to the deys of Algiers, Tunis and Tripoli that she would pay them large sums in tribute each year if they would prevent the seizure of English ships—but English ships only. Spain did the same thing in the hope of protecting her own shipping. So did other nations.

The deys found all these offers very attractive. They accepted tribute from each country, and then permitted the piracy of their subjects to go on more or less as before. The deys became incredibly rich on pirate loot. More treasure was heaped up in Algiers, people said, from pirate raids and tribute payment, than could be found in any other city of the world. When the United States established herself as a new nation, at the end of the American Revolution, the deys demanded tribute from America, too.

The American government, shocked and angered at the demands, nevertheless duly paid tribute at first, because it felt too weak to do anything else. In 1789, for example, it sent the Dey of Algiers twenty-six barrels of silver dollars.

But in 1804, when authorities in the city of Tripoli seized the grounded American ship *Philadelphia*, and dragged her crew off to prison, young Lieutenant Stephen Decatur managed to lead a party aboard the captured vessel. He sought to destroy her, and hoped that the explosion he made would wreck the whole city. It didn't. However, the episode won lasting fame for young Decatur, and proved that the Americans didn't intend to go on paying tribute for ever. Soon armed American ships were sailing boldly up to one pirate port after another, to issue ultimatums to the deys.

To the Dey of Algiers, for example, Decatur sent word that Americans would pay no more tribute. He demanded the return of all slaves captured from American ships, together with compensation for damage done to their shipping. If the Dey refused to accept the ultimatum, Decatur added, his ships' cannon would blow Algiers to bits. Within a matter of hours the startled Dey agreed to Decatur's terms.

Tunis and Tripoli gave in just as easily to the energetic and confident young country which dared to treat Moslem rulers as criminals instead of meekly giving in to their highhandedness. To this day the victory over the Barbary Coast is a proud chapter in American naval history, and Marines still sing of American courage on "the shores of Tripoli."

THE EUROPEAN "GRAB" BEGINS

By 1815 or thereabouts the Barbary pirates were making what proved to be their last raids. But in a way it was the American Revolution, even more than American naval power, which paved the road for their downfall. The American Revolution cut the United States off from Europe, and so the European powers turned their eyes toward the Mediterranean again.

Napoleon made a triumphal entry into Egypt in 1798 and claimed it in the name of France. Turkey, which owned Egypt then, hastily sought England's help. The French appetite for holdings in North Africa grew even though Napoleon was defeated. France announced that piracy could no longer be allowed to flourish in the Mediterranean—that the Barbary pirates must be subdued.

Other nations quickly announced that they too were against piracy. This really meant that the new land grab for North Africa was about to begin.

France was the chief victor in the struggle that

suddenly got under way for all of North Africa. She had to fight—or make deals—with England, Turkey and Italy, as well as the North Africans themselves, and she had to yield some of her claims in other parts of the continent. But once she set seriously about the job of bringing the bulk of North Africa under her control, she didn't stop until the job was done. It took her a little less than a century. Independent North Africa ceased to be.

In 1830 France took Algiers, claimed the territory around it—the whole country now called Algeria, including the Sahara—and made it an official part of France.

It was a strong first move. It established her squarely in the middle of the North African coastline. Next she turned eastward, and in 1881 took over Tunisia to "protect" it from a threatened Italian invasion.

Morocco, to the west of the new French province of Algeria, was the final goal of the French campaign, and the hardest to win. But in 1912 France and Spain agreed to "protect" the land jointly, and they set up what they called French Morocco and Spanish Morocco side by side.

The only part of North Africa that didn't fall into French hands (except for Spanish Morocco) was the broad stretch of desert lying between Tunisia and Egypt. Until 1912 Turkey more or less controlled that area, and until that date it was divided into three ancient provinces called Tripolitania, Fezzan and Cyrenaica. Then, in that year, those provinces were conquered by Italy and combined into a single Italian colony called Libya.

So, by 1912, all four North African countries were brought under the control of European powers. And European mastery, it seemed, would last for ever.

But this was not to be. Morocco, Tunisia and Libya had all become free, independent nations by 1956. European rule in these countries only lasted —amazingly enough—for about forty years. Algeria is still, it is true, part of France and under French control, but it has been struggling for freedom too, and it may not be part of France indefinitely.

The story of the sensational contemporary evolution of North Africa toward independence is so dramatic and important that we must deal with each country separately and in detail. But first let us look at some of the great forces, issues and ideas common to the region as a whole, and binding it together.

2

What North Africans Believe In

ISLAM, the Moslem religion that stimulated one of
the world's greatest waves of conquest thirteen hundred years ago, has grown tremendously since then.
Today there are about four hundred million Moslems in the world. And North Africa's people are
overwhelmingly Moslem. Ninety per cent of all
Moroccans, Algerians, Tunisians and Libyans follow
the teaching of Mohammed, the Prophet of Allah,
as set forth in their sacred book, the Koran.

We should have another word about this fascinating man.

Mohammed was born in the city of Mecca, on the
Arabian Peninsula, about the year 570. His family
belonged to a tribe of pagan Arabs called Koreish,
and during his boyhood he was a shepherd. But at
the age of twenty-four Mohammed went to work
for a wealthy widow named Khadija, and this gave
him the chance to travel with caravans carrying on
trade with distant cities. During those journeys he
met Jews and Christians for the first time, and
learned something about their religions.

A little later Mohammed married Khadija and settled down as a highly respected businessman in Mecca. He became especially well known for his wisdom in settling quarrels and disputes. But, in spite of his good fortune and fine reputation, he wasn't happy. He began to spend a great deal of time in a cave outside the city, where, alone, he sought to solve the problems troubling him.

He came to feel that the idol worship of his tribesmen was somehow wrong. Instead, he decided, he himself wanted to worship the one God of the Jews and the Christians. But he also thought the Jews and Christians themselves had strayed away from the teaching of the early prophets like Abraham. There ought to be, Mohammed felt, some new and simpler way to worship the God the Jews and Christians called Jehovah.

But when Mohammed began to preach the worship of Allah, which was his name for the conception of God he developed, outside of his own small family and circle of friends, he ran into trouble. Tribesmen grew angry at him for attacking their pagan gods. The businessmen of Mecca resented him too. Mecca was then a holy city for pagans, and thousands of Arabs visited it each year to worship the hundreds of idols set up in the temple of Al Ka'aba. Looking after those pilgrims—feeding and housing them, selling them souvenirs and stabling their camels—was a profitable business, like the tourist business around popular shrines in many other countries. And Mecca businessmen were afraid the business would be ruined if Mohammed persuaded people to stop worshipping those idols.

So Mohammed and some fifty converts finally left Mecca and settled at a little oasis that later became the important city of Medina. This journey to Medina, in the year 622—usually called The Flight, or Hegira—marks the beginning of the Moslem calendar, just as the coming of Christ marks the beginning of the Christian calendar.

Mohammed's converts multiplied rapidly in his new home. He and his people were able to defend themselves against an army sent against them from Mecca. He successfully fought hostile tribes in the neighbourhood too, tribes of both Jewish and pagan beliefs. Eight years after his arrival in Medina he decided to conquer Mecca itself. But his fame had spread so widely by then that his native city gave up to him without a blow.

Mohammed entered Mecca in triumph and destroyed all 360 of the pagan idols in the temple of Al Ka'aba. The temple itself he left standing. He considered it sacred because it was believed to have been built by Abraham, and Mohammed revered Abraham just as he revered Moses and Jesus.

From that time on Mecca was a holy city for Moslems, just as it had once been a holy pagan city. And, as it turned out, the pilgrim business flourished from then on even more than it had done in the past. To this day thousands of Moslems make a pilgrimage to Mecca every year.

Mohammed died in 632, and after his death his faithful followers wrote down all the sentences that make up the Koran, sentences which until then Mohammed and his converts had recited to each other. They also set down the hundreds of other statements made by Mohammed during his busy life, and those became the laws and regulations known as the Sunna. The Koran and the Sunna form the foundation of what we call Islam.

Let us try to describe and analyse this strange, dynamic faith. The appeal of Islam is very simple and direct. There are no ministers, no priests, no rabbis. Moslems can pray anywhere—on the roadside, in a factory or in a field, riding in a caravan or travelling in a plane. Usually each man prays alone. Only at noon on Friday do the faithful collect in a common gathering place called in Arabic a *masjid*. In English our word for it is mosque.

A mosque is generally a square or rectangular structure built around a courtyard, and some of them are brightly decorated with tiles and carvings. Three sides are formed by roofed-over corridors, or arcades, without any inner walls. The fourth side, the one that faces Mecca, contains the prayer room with its domed roof. If the mosque has a minaret, or tower, it may stand at one end of this fourth side.

Five times a day—at sunrise, at noon, in the afternoon, at sunset and at dusk—a man climbs to the top of the mosque's minaret, or stands in the doorway if the mosque has no tower, and summons all faithful Moslems to prayer. He repeats his call four times, each time facing a different point of the compass. Called a muezzin, he is chosen for this task because he has a pleasant voice strong enough to carry for a long distance—though some mosques now have loudspeakers.

Moslems remove their shoes at the door of the

2

mosque, in order to preserve the purity of the building. (This purity would also be defiled by the presence of Christians or Jews. That's why most mosques are closed to all but Moslems.) As soon as the faithful enter the courtyard, they wash their hands, faces and feet in the pool at its centre. Then they move on to the prayer room and take up positions in rows facing a small niche, called a *milrah*, which indicates the direction of Mecca. There are rugs on the floor of the prayer room, but no pews or seats of any kind.

The Friday prayers are usually led by a prayer leader, or imam. Like the muezzin, he has no higher religious standing than other Moslems. He is usually appointed to his office because of his wisdom and his knowledge of the prayer ritual. But a mosque doesn't always have a regular imam. The prayer leader may be chosen each time from among those who have gathered at the mosque.

The imam stands at the head of the group, facing Mecca. Those who have come to pray stand behind him, facing in the same direction, and copy his words and movements as he goes through the ritual —first standing erect, then bowing, then kneeling, then sitting back on his heels, then bending forward to touch his forehead to the ground, and finally rising again. Then, to conclude the ceremony, the imam may give a brief talk, often about community affairs.

THE FIVE PILLARS OF ISLAM

There are five principal duties which every Moslem is expected to perform:

   1. He must declare that there is no God but Allah, and that Mohammed is His Messenger.

   2. He must pray five times a day, facing Mecca.

   3. He must contribute to charity about 10 per cent of his annual income. This sum, called *zakah*, may be given directly to the poor or sick, or to one of the many funds for aiding the poor, building hospitals, digging wells or supporting other worthy projects. (This practice is by no means strictly observed by all Moslems today.)

   4. He must fast between dawn and dusk every day during the entire month of Ramadan, the ninth month of the Arabic calendar.

   5. He must make, if possible, at least one pilgrimage to Mecca during his lifetime. A Moslem who has made this pilgrimage adds the title "hadj" to his name and wears a green turban, so that all may recognize his right to the title at a glance.

Moslems who faithfully carry out all these duties are promised a life after death in paradise. There, the Koran says, in a garden filled with all the beautiful things any man could desire, the lowliest beggar and the richest ruler will be equal. In paradise all Moslems will be happy, no matter how miserable they may have been on earth.

Everything that happens on earth, most Moslems believe, whether it is good or bad, is the will of Allah. That's why a common word heard in all Moslem countries is *inshallah*, which means "If God wills it." Ask a Moslem if he thinks it will rain tomorrow, or if his crops are going to be good this year, and he will probably answer "*Inshallah.*"

One reason for the rapid adoption of Islam, during the days when it was spreading like wildfire over so much of the world, is that it makes no distinction between races. There is no bar to the conversion of Asians or Negroes, for example. There are probably ten million Moslems in Nigeria, a black African country, alone.

In fact, Islam has been called the most democratic of the world's great religions. Even the absence of pews or seats in a mosque is one illustration of this. If a mosque had pews, Moslems think, men of wealth or high position might be tempted to reserve the best for themselves. In the mosque—as in the eyes of God—all Moslems consider themselves equal, and all consider themselves better than any non-Moslem.

Another reason for the rapid spread of Islam is that it permits its followers to hold on to ancient tribal beliefs. Many Moslems—perhaps the majority —believe not only in Islam, but also in the assorted spirits, holy men and superstitions popular in their own neighbourhood.

Most of us have heard, for example, of djinns or genies, like the one that appeared suddenly whenever Aladdin rubbed his magic lamp. To us they seem to be mere figures in fairy stories, but to many Moslems they are not fairy-tale characters at all. They are very real creatures to be reckoned with in daily life.

A great many marabouts, or holy men, have also built up wide followings among Moslems who revere them for their deep faith and good deeds. A marabout is supposed to have *baraka*, a mystical God-given quality usually difficult for Westerners to understand. A man who possesses *baraka* is believed to have the ability to bless people, and sometimes the power to foretell the future.

To touch a marabout, or even to be near him, is considered highly beneficial. His home or his tomb may even become a shrine where people come to ask favours. A shrine of this kind is also called a marabout, and there are hundreds of them in North Africa.

MOHAMMED WAS PRACTICAL

The Koran and the Sunna contain many examples of Mohammed's practical common sense. Mohammed thought, for example, that Arabs drank too much, so he forbade the drinking of any alcoholic beverage. This is one reason, by the way, for the popularity of non-alcoholic soft drinks like Coca-Cola in North Africa today.

Mohammed also prohibited the eating of pork, probably because he was aware that meat spoils rapidly in hot countries, and also, perhaps, because he thought Arabs would be better off if they raised sheep and goats instead of pigs. As a herdsman he knew that sheep and goats—unlike pigs—could graze even on sparse desert pasturage and yield milk and wool as well as meat.

Mohammed thought that many Arabs, especially

among the city dwellers, got too little exercise. He therefore invented a prayer ritual which called for a good deal of activity in the form of bending and kneeling.

He knew that the Arabs of his time were careless about cleanliness, so he insisted that every Moslem wash before praying—which meant that all Moslems had to wash at least five times a day. But the Koran adds that Moslems travelling through waterless regions may "wash" with sand instead of water.

An important thing to remember about Mohammed's statements is that some of them are open to different interpretations, just as certain parts of the Bible are, or, in a secular field, parts of the Constitution of the United States. For example, the Koran forbids the making of images, either of men or of animals. That's why Moslems have no paintings or statues of their famous caliphs of the past. But nowadays some Moslems do have their pictures taken.

A WORD ABOUT WOMEN AND MARRIAGE

Today, as in the past, women occupy an inferior and restricted position in the Moslem world, but the Moslem religion is by no means entirely to blame for this. The Koran doesn't say, for example, that women should be veiled, or that they should live in a part of the house separate from the men. Those are both old Arab customs that have nothing to do with the Moslem faith. Many Berber women, who are

Moslems, don't wear veils at all. And though it is true that Moslem women are seldom seen in a mosque—many never leave their homes at all— there is nothing in the Koran that prevents them from going to the mosque to pray just as their husbands do.

On the whole the Koran improved the position of women in the Arab world. Before Mohammed's day they were little better than slaves, and some tribes even buried girl babies alive to get rid of them. Mohammed condemned the murder of girl babies, and the Koran gives women certain definite rights. It permits them to have wealth of their own, and to become teachers, writers and traders. It assures a wife part of her husband's estate when he dies.

The Koran does say that a man may have as many as four wives at a time. This fact is so widely known that polygamy, or the practice of having more than one wife, is sometimes thought to be a Moslem invention. It isn't, of course. It was common among Arabs and many other peoples much earlier, and has also been common in several non-Moslem parts of the world. (In the United States it was practised until not too long ago by the Mormons, as we all know.)

In fact many Arabs had more than four wives before Mohammed's day, and found the rule of the Koran quite harsh—especially as it told them they must treat all their wives exactly alike. This meant that if a man gave his first wife a house and servants, he had to give the second—and third and fourth— the same.

But the Koran did make it easy for men to have

several wives, one after the other. It made it easy, in other words, for a man to divorce a wife. He could accomplish this by simply appearing before a Koranic court and stating three times, "I divorce thee." Mohammed himself married eleven times, and one of his grandsons married and divorced a hundred wives.

The position of women is changing today in North Africa—changing rapidly in some places, more slowly in others. One of the most striking changes is that polygamy is going out of fashion. In the farming areas, where a man's wives work in the fields, he may still have three or four wives because they earn their keep. But in the cities—more and more Moslems tend to live in cities nowadays—wives cost money, and only the wealthy can afford more than one.

Girls are being educated in North Africa today, too. Not very many of them go to school yet. In fact, Moslem boys going to school in Morocco, as an example, outnumber girls five hundred to one. But a few women at least are being equipped these days for a new kind of life, and are eager to see something of the world outside their homes. Some of them even manage to see an American film now and then. (In some Moslem areas, Arab women are still forbidden to go to films of any kind.)

A Moslem girl, especially one who has had a little education, seldom wants to be one of four wives nowadays. She prefers to have a husband and family all to herself. She may even think—this is a very unusual idea for North Africa—that she has the right to meet a young man before she marries him, and to be in love with him. This is startling because the usual practice is for marriages to be arranged by the parents, without any consultation at all with the youngsters. As a rule, a Moslem girl has never even laid eyes on her bridegroom until the moment of the wedding.

Of course there are not very many "modern" young women as yet, and they usually have a hard time of it. Even if their own parents encourage them, they may be frowned upon by everyone else. Moslem boys of "good families" will probably be afraid to associate with them. It will be a long time still before twenty-year-old Ahmed can invite eighteen-year-old Fatima to have a cup of coffee with him, or to go for a ride in the moonlight. But a small beginning has been made in that direction.

Just how small that beginning is I realized when I suddenly walked into a Moslem wedding procession in a mountain village in Morocco. I was clambering through the pale rocky alleys of this little town, looking at its pretty mosques in pastel colours, when I first heard musicians playing shrill pipes and beating rude drums shaped like tambourines.

Behind the musicians came bearded elders of the bride's family, and a woman in a red-and-white striped cloth bearing large green and yellow candles. Next came more musicians, and then a group of eight panting youths carrying a paper box on long poles.

This box was not very big. It was shaped like a hat, or narrow tent, square at the bottom and pointed at the top. But it was clearly heavy. The boys were bent under its weight. In a torrent of coloured silk streamers, they disappeared with it down the road. Concealed inside was the bride. I guessed that she was probably plump, because I knew she would have been fattened up for the ceremony. To be plump is to be fashionable in North Africa. But I couldn't guess whether she had the small nose, small mouth and big eyes that would mean she was regarded as beautiful.

This was all I saw of the ceremony. Nobody sees much more. The bride was being carried to the groom's home, where she would meet him—for the very first time! The marriage had been arranged by the elders in both families, and the bride had been purchased for a price agreed upon among them.

I was told that the bride and groom would eat a wedding feast together, and that it might be the last meal they would have together for the rest of their lives. After the wedding night the bride would eat with only the women of her household, and she might never leave the house after she had entered it. Once a year—perhaps—her mother might call on her. Once a year—perhaps—she might be allowed to visit a sister or a female cousin. For the rest of the time she would be, in effect, her husband's servant, perpetually kept out of sight in the harem or elsewhere.

If she had sons, they would be welcomed. But daughters would be lamented. Most of North Africa is still very much a man's world!

3

The Peoples of North Africa

THERE is an old Arab saying, "A Berber is not a true Moslem, but only thinks he is." And it is a fact that Berbers aren't always "true Moslems" by Arab standards. Many Berbers eat pork, for example, although the Koran forbids it. But the old saying suggests more than that. It suggests the wide difference that still exists between the two groups of people who make up the bulk of North Africa's population today.

Arabs and Berbers have intermingled to some extent, but, generally speaking, the two groups live apart, live quite differently and still don't like each other. Arabs tend to be desert nomads or to live as workers in towns, whereas the Berbers are farmers out in the hills. Arabs are, by and large, apt to be darker-skinned than Berbers, although some Berbers intermingled with Negro slaves in the old days and may be dark as well.

Berbers today make up about half of Libya's population, nearly one-half of Morocco's, and nearly one-third of Algeria's, but there are not many left in

Tunisia. Most of them still live, as they have for centuries, in small farming villages. Their houses are usually small and made of sun-dried brick, and are almost bare of furniture. Berbers naturally sit on the ground to talk or eat or work. They have no need for tables or chairs.

A Berber still gives his strongest loyalty to his tribe. Ask him who he is and he almost never says, "I am a Moroccan," or "I come from the city of Marrakesh." Instead he answers proudly, "I belong to such-and-such a tribe." His caid and his pasha command his complete allegiance in most cases. (A caid is, more or less, a rural magistrate or leader of a tribe. A pasha is a provincial governor, or head of a municipal administration, and may thus be the leader of a whole group of tribes.)

During the early years of the French occupation of Morocco, for example, a whole army of Berbers fought fiercely on the French side—because their pasha was friendly to France. They even fought against other Berbers who were trying to drive off the French invaders.

As fighters, brandishing ancient muskets, they showed magnificent bravery and spirit. They seem to enjoy fighting, unlike Arabs. Arabs are apt to become hysterical at the sight of blood, hate to fight with their hands—they use knives if necessary—and draw back even from a hearty handshake in order to protect their usually delicate fingers. The Berbers are tougher and don't have this dislike of physical contact. The French, who despised most Arabs, often said admiringly, "Berbers are *men*!"

Except for the group called the Tuareg—we'll

meet them in the Sahara—the Berbers have never had a written language. They have no literature, no newspapers, no textbooks. Some Berbers speak Arabic, of course, but by no means all. And those who don't may spend their whole lives, even today, without knowing very much of what goes on in the cities where North Africa's modern history is being made.

This gives the Arabs a further reason to look down on the Berbers. Arabs say Berbers are too backward and uneducated to play a part in the building of their new up-and-coming nations.

THE ARABS

Some Arabs are still desert dwellers, wandering about in the arid regions south of the Atlas Mountains. But Arabs also form the largest part of almost every North African city's population, and more Arabs are moving to the cities every year.

On the whole they are better educated than Berbers, more progressive-minded. It was the Arabs who were most active in the political movements that demanded and won national independence from France. Arabs now fill most of the native-held government posts in those newly independent countries. Many Arabs, in other words, are what we call "nationalists." The Arabs of Tunisia, for example, no longer even speak of themselves as Arabs. They call themselves Tunisians.

Arabs today are desperately eager for education, because they know that this is the road to progress.

Under French control they had few schools. A French official in Morocco once told me, during the period of French administration, that Arabs couldn't be educated. It was impossible, he said, to make an Arab into a good lawyer or engineer. Of course this is nonsense. The reason the French didn't want the Arabs to be educated was that they feared education would lead to independence. When Arabs get the chance to go to school, they learn all sorts of professions.

Well-educated Arabs, incidentally, don't always choose to adopt Western-style clothes. Many of them still prefer their native garments, partly from pride, perhaps, partly because they are so handsome and comfortable.

The basic garment worn by Arabs—and by Berbers too—is a kind of long gown with a hood. This is not only cool in warm weather, but also warm when the weather is cool. It keeps out dust and sand, and is at once coat, hat, robe, overcoat, blanket and pyjamas. Sometimes a burnoose, a larger hooded cloak, is also worn. When an Arab sleeps outdoors, he turns his burnoose upside down and put his feet in the hood.

Even an Arab who wears European-cut suits, however, may still insist that his wife and daughters wear veils and never appear in public. That's why most Arab women are still draped from head to toe in the traditional white wrapper they have worn for centuries. But of course a very wealthy woman may wear a Paris dress or suit under her white wrapper.

Certain traits are supposed to be peculiarly Arab. I have heard, for example, that Arabs are particu-

larly cruel and that they can be treacherous liars.
I have also heard that an Arab will do anything to
a building rather than repair it. He will patch—but
not repair. And an old proverb says, "An Arab is a
man who will pull down a whole temple to have a
stone to sit on."

But it is also true that Arabs can be skilled handicraft workers. The saying is that nobody in the
world can rival an Arab for doing delicate work with
a chisel—held between his toes! And there is no
doubt that today more and more Arabs are driving
cars, operating lathes and learning many of the
complicated processes of modern industrial life.

Another Arab trait is that they are deeply democratic in their personal instincts, and have fanatic
loyalty to their friends and their own kind. That's
why they feel a sense of kinship with all other Moslems everywhere.

SPEAKING AND WRITING ARABIC

Arabic is really a whole lot of languages, just as
English is. A man who can speak one brand, or
dialect, may not be able to understand others—just
as a resident of rural Somerset may not easily
understand a Scotsman.

Most Arab-speaking people of North Africa can
follow each other's speech pretty well, however, even
if one from far-western Morocco may have difficulty
following the speech of far-eastern Libya.

But written Arabic is the same everywhere, and an

educated Arab of Morocco can read newspapers or books printed in every other Arab-speaking country.

Arabic is written from right to left, like Hebrew —not from left to right, like English. And in its written form it is a sort of shorthand. For example, the Arabic word for hill or mountain, *jebel*, is written in Arabic as *jbl*. It's as if we wrote the English words, *man speaking*, as *mn spkng*.

When these shorthand Arabic words are said out loud, the unwritten letters—the vowels—are filled in by the speaker. Several people may therefore pronounce *jbl* in several different ways. This is one reason why it's difficult to write down an Arabic word in such a way that English-speaking people will pronounce it correctly. Another reason is that there are some Arabic sounds which we cannot duplicate exactly with the letters of our own alphabet.

This shorthand system used in Arabic writing also explains why Arabic is difficult for English-speaking people to learn. All of us, perhaps, could easily memorize the fact that the three letters *ktb* mean "to do with writing." But those three letters—or that root word, as we might call it—are the basis for dozens of other words, and they are not so easy to remember. Here are just a few of the words based on *ktb*, spelled out more or less the way they sound in Arabic:

maktub	something written
katib	writer
kitabat	writing
kaataba	to write
seyektub	will write soon
yektub	will write later

Because of this same shorthand system there are at least a dozen ways to spell the name of the Prophet Mohammed in English. Probably the most correct form is Muḥammad, with—you will notice—a small dot under the *h*. The name Mohammed, incidentally, is almost as popular among Arabs as the name John is among English-speaking people.

The word Moslem is written in several ways too. In books published in England it generally appears as *Muslim*, and French-speaking people usually call a Moslem a *musulman*, with a small *m*.

NORTH AFRICA'S NEGROES

Three other groups of people—Negroes, Jews and Europeans—make up the rest of North Africa's population. None of these three groups is anywhere near as large as the Berber and Arab groups.

Probably the Negroes are the least numerous of all—I say "probably" because North African statistics are not very reliable. At any rate I had to go deep into the Sahara before I saw a town with a population that was predominantly Negro.

Negroes in North Africa were brought into the land originally as slaves, and some were not freed until thirty or forty years ago. And, being slaves, they had no reason to learn anything. They understood nothing but words of command. Hence, they are still largely uneducated.

But Negroes may play a far different and more productive role in North Africa's future. A chance at education can lead to many things. Besides, there are enormous Negro populations in central and western Africa who are today winning a new place in the world. And, as those people gain in power and influence, it seems likely that the Negroes of North Africa will share in their gains.

THE JEWS OF NORTH AFRICA

Altogether probably half a million or more Jews now live in North Africa, most of them in Morocco. And this is one place in the world where Jews and Arabs have, until recently, managed to get on together tolerably well. But nowadays the events of modern history—and the Moslem religion—are tending to drive them apart.

Among North Africa's Jews are many who arrived there during the last century, with other colonists from France, Italy and Spain. These people generally think of themselves as Europeans rather than as Jews. But also there are much older colonies of Jews scattered here and there—colonies that have been in existence for hundreds of years—and they are likely to be intensely Jewish in feeling. One of the oldest, on the island of Djerba off the coast of Tunisia, has been established for nineteen hundred years.

Some North African Jews are quite well-to-do; some are bitterly poor. In the city of Tangier in Morocco, for example, the descendants of Jews who came from Spain in the fifteenth century form a privileged and wealthy class. But there are also Jews living in villages behind the Atlas Mountains in conditions of the utmost misery and squalor.

Jews were usually made welcome in North African cities in the past because they were skilled craftsmen —jewellers and tailors, especially—and because they were willing, or could be forced, to perform services which Moslems couldn't or wouldn't perform for themselves. One of those services, in the days of the old sultans, was grisly. Jewish butchers were compelled to pickle in salt the heads of men executed by the sultans' orders, so that those heads could be put up for public display. This is why, today, the Jewish quarter of a Moroccan city is still called the *mellah*. The word means "salt" in Arabic.

Jews also became the bankers and moneylenders of North Africa, because the Koran forbids Moslems —in theory—to charge interest on borrowed money. And, as bankers, of course, they wielded considerable influence. This situation may change in the future, however, because wealthy Moslems, eager to invest in North Africa's new industries, are beginning to ignore the Koran's ban on charging interest.

THE EUROPEANS

Until recently the most powerful group of people in North Africa was one of the smallest—the *colons*, or European colonists who had gone there to settle from their homelands in Europe. Most of these were French. Others came from Spain, Italy and the islands of Sicily and Corsica. Altogether they numbered less than two million, out of North Africa's total population of more than twenty-three million. But the colons were the bosses. They ran most of North Africa and ran it pretty much as they pleased, until they began to be forced out by the power of the new nationalist movements.

The French colons in French Morocco, for example, owned an enormous share of all the land that could be profitably cultivated—while hundreds of thousands of Moroccans had no land at all, and worked for miserable wages on the colons' farms. The colons also held practically every post in the government. They wouldn't even permit an Arab to serve as a postmaster for the purely Arab quarter of a Moroccan city. Practically every engineer, lawyer, doctor, hotel proprietor, manicurist, barman or salesgirl in a good shop came from France.

In their own opinion, of course, the colons were transforming a backward land into a modern one. They were proud of the roads they built, the public-health system they set up, the mines they opened, the factories they constructed. They felt that the native population should look up to them as natural leaders. And of course they looked down on the natives. When Frenchmen spoke to Arabs they used the kind of language that would be spoken to a child or a servant. Behind the Arabs' backs they used terms they had coined especially for the purpose, by running words together. They called the Arabs the *salerace*, meaning "dirty people," or *salesarabes*, meaning "dirty Arabs."

They saw nothing wrong in this attitude. When I

tried to discuss it with them, they reproached me instead for the way Americans treated Indians in the old days and treat Negroes now. The colons had a point, of course. Many countries still have a long way to go in some matters that have to do with race, even if they have made a great deal of progress recently.

In any case, the North Africans themselves came to hate the colons more and more. They resented everything about them—even while they envied them their wealth and influence—and in particular regarded them as foreign oppressors. Nor did Arabs or Berbers like to be referred to as "dirty people" or to be called by the French word for natives, which is *indigènes*. (They don't like our word *natives* either, and I am using it only when it seems necessary for clarity.) They like to be called "Africans" or by the name of their country.

Strong resentment against the colons finally led North Africans to feel that they would rather rule themselves—even if they did so badly at first—than be ruled, and exploited, by foreigners. And it was this feeling that gave rise to the fight for independence which has been the outstanding event in the modern history of Morocco, Tunisia, Algeria and Libya.

4

The Wonderful World of Morocco

MOROCCO today is smoking and crackling with the heat of friction—friction between the ancient and the modern. Its brand-new independence strikes sparks against age-old traditions. Western clothes brush against the flowing Arab robes, called *djellabas*. Camels and donkeys, moving at their accustomed slow pace, compete with noisy speeding trucks and buses.

This same kind of friction exists all over North Africa, of course. But it seems sharpest of all in Morocco, perhaps because of the country's geography.

Morocco's 170,000 square miles—its area is almost six times that of Scotland—is tucked away on Africa's northwest rim. It faces in two directions, with a coastline that looks toward Europe on one side of the Strait of Gibraltar, and toward the Western hemisphere on the other. And the mountains that run parallel to the coast—the high ranges of the Atlas—have cut it off to some extent from the rest of Africa.

The Turks, for example, powerful enough to

conquer all of Morocco's eastern neighbours, never pushed past those mountains to take Morocco itself. Even the ebb and flow of the Arab conquest, sweeping back and forth over most of North Africa for centuries, didn't always reach this westernmost of all Moslem countries. And though today there is a strong European—and American—influence in such coastal cities as Tangier and Casablanca, this seldom penetrated beyond the mountains.

This is why contrasts in Morocco today are so striking. No two buildings could look less alike than, say, a glittering new apartment house in Casablanca and a tribal mud castle deep in the Atlas.

And that's why so much of Morocco seems isolated and shut off from the rest of the world. I have visited every Islamic country on the globe except two, but I have never felt such a dense, closed-in feeling as in Morocco.

The same mountains that separate Morocco from the rest of North Africa also tend to divide its population into two groups: those who live in the cities and the plains, and those who live in the towering mountains themselves.

The Arabs, together with the people of mixed Arab-Berber descent, form most of the first—and much larger—group. They number about six million. Morocco's cities and plains are also the home of most of its three hundred thousand or so French colons and of about a hundred thousand other settlers of European stock, including most of the Jews.

The Berber stronghold is the hard-to-reach mountain region. There are about three million Berbers who are divided into no fewer than 375 different tribes or subtribes. As I have already indicated, these rugged folk have always relished their isolation and freedom. Few Moroccan sultans ever gained any authority over them—which meant that few sultans ruled over more than one-quarter of Morocco.

Now, even though we have already described briefly some aspects of the history of North Africa in general, we should have a few words specifically about Moroccan history. It is necessary in the understanding of today's story.

Late in the eighth century the Arab world, stretching between Syria and Spain, began to break off in bits and pieces. That was when Idris, that energetic descendant of the Prophet Mohammed, quarrelled with the caliph of the day. By 788 he had established a court in the old Roman town of Volubilis, near the present city of Meknes, and proclaimed himself Sultan of a new Moroccan empire—an empire that has existed ever since.

Idris died shortly afterward, poisoned by an agent of the angry caliph. Sudden and violent death was the fate of many sultans who followed him. Their lives and reigns were frequently rather short. And many candidates for the throne died before they could reach it—which is not surprising when we know how those sultans were chosen. The throne of Morocco didn't pass automatically from father to eldest son, but went to any male member of the royal family selected by a group of holy men gathered in the city of Fez.

This conclave, known as the Ulema of Fez, was

one of Islam's holiest institutions—comparable to the College of Cardinals in Rome, which chooses the popes of the Roman Catholic Church. When the Ulema named a new sultan it was, in fact, much like naming a pope, because Morocco's sultan is also the supreme head of the country's church. In theory, the Ulema always chose—from among all the ex-sultan's relatives—the one best fitted to serve his people as both their religious leader and their lawmaker.

This theory did not always work out in practice, and rivalry among members of a ruling family, or between two powerful families, caused a rapid turnover of Moroccan sultans. In the period from 788 to 1912 Morocco had altogether 115 rulers, and they belonged to nine different families, or dynasties. Six were Berber and three were Arab. The present ruler, an Arab, belongs to the Sherifian dynasty which has been in power since 1688. The official name of Morocco—before it became the modern kingdom of Morocco—was the Sherifian Empire.

When European nations got busy carving up Africa the Sherifians began to worry about their future—naturally. One sultan even went so far as to ask the United States (in 1870) to establish a protectorate over Morocco. But the United States, occupied in opening up its own western territory, wasn't interested in Africa. So the field was left open for France, which had been eyeing Morocco for some time.

France didn't try to conquer the country openly by force of arms. World opinion, even then, might have been shocked by outright, overt invasion. France adopted a different scheme—a series of deals with other European powers. She promised England a free hand in Egypt, if England wouldn't interfere with her in Morocco, and made similar arrangements with Germany and Italy. She also bought off Spain by promising Spain a share in the Moroccan loot, if any.

The perfect moment for French intervention came in 1912. Then, suddenly, the Sultan was besieged in Fez, his capital, by thousands of Berbers eager to remove him from office. All France had to do was to respond to the Sultan's appeal for help. The French sent an army to Fez, lifted the siege and announced that from that time on she would "protect" the country in order to save the Sultan further trouble from his unruly subjects.

When the episode was over Morocco found itself divided into three parts. They were known as French Morocco, Spanish Morocco and the International Zone of Tangier.

France held the lion's share, about 90 per cent of the country's territory and population. That is, she held it theoretically. Actually many Moroccan cities and towns fought back against the French and had to be subdued one by one. In fact, fighting went on against the newcomers, especially in the hills south of the Atlas, for more than twenty years. It would even be true to say that France never really "pacified" all of French Morocco.

Spanish Morocco, a much smaller area, covered only the northeastern rim of the country, but it too was not completely subdued for a long, long time. Moroccans are stubborn people.

The third division, the city of Tangier, occupied

the point of land overlooking the Strait of Gibraltar, gateway to the Mediterranean. This strategic spot had already been made an international community ruled jointly by several nations. Those nations had come to this agreement because all of them, jealous of each other, were afraid of letting the city fall into the hands of any single European country. And now, under the new scheme of division, France and Spain were both afraid to upset that arrangement.

THE FRENCH RULE IN MOROCCO

The story of Morocco from 1912 until it became independent in 1956 is chiefly the story of the rule of the French.

For the first thirteen years of this period one man handled two tremendous jobs—governing Morocco and subduing it. He was Louis Hubert Gonzalve Lyautey, usually spoken of as Marshal Lyautey. His official title was that of Resident General, and his Residency became the real seat of Moroccan government. He is one of the greatest administrators in colonial history.

Lyautey, as it happened, loved Morocco and the Moroccans, and deeply respected their traditions. As a result he was able to win the admiration of men who at first hated him as a stranger and a conqueror.

Lyautey's feeling about his job showed itself very early in his career. One day he rode on horseback into the city of Rabat—the coastal city he had chosen as the French capital—and saw French workmen busily engaged in putting up the new Residency buildings and others intended to serve as government offices. The new buildings were going up in the heart of the old Arab town.

Marshal Lyautey stiffened in his saddle. "Tear those down at once," he commanded.

Those five words were enough. With them Lyautey established the policy followed rigidly from then on: no new French buildings would be erected where they would disrupt an old Arab town. Instead, by Lyautey's order, they formed a new and separate quarter of their own. Because of this policy Moroccan cities even now are sharply divided into Arab and French quarters, with two parallel communities existing side by side.

Lyautey showed his skill as a colonial governor by inventing the policy of "co-sovereignty," a system by which he and the Moroccan Sultan appeared to rule the country together. Lyautey actually made all the rules and regulations, but when they were issued they appeared in the form of decrees signed by the Sultan—just as if he had thought them up himself. This discouraged revolt among people who would have grown angry if they thought that their Sultan was being humiliated by the French newcomer.

Lyautey also believed, quite sensibly, that there was no reason for him to destroy the ancient rituals and tribal rules that people had followed for generations. Instead he used those rituals and practices as instruments of French control. He didn't take away a tribal chief's power, for example; he made that chief a kind of subgovernor under his own authority, and in this way won the chief's loyalty and the loyalty of the tribe as well.

This system worked easily and well, on the whole, among the Arabs. The Berbers were a different matter. Some of the tribes back in the hills had never recognized the authority of the Sultan, and now had no intention of recognizing French authority either. So Lyautey went to work to win over, one by one, the caids and pashas who ruled the Berber tribes.

One man in particular, the Pasha of Marrakesh, went over to the French at the very beginning. The French never had a more faithful or more powerful ally. This man, Hadj Thami Glaoui et Mezourari—usually called simply El Glaoui—was a picturesque old chieftain and one of the most remarkable characters I ever met. He boasted about how many men he had killed with his own hand, during the 121 battles he fought during his youth. But he was also a graceful, sophisticated gentleman with great political experience—and perhaps the last feudal lord on earth with a private "army." His Berber warriors numbered three hundred thousand.

El Glaoui was never an outright French puppet. He worked with the French because he really liked them. He was French administrator for much of southern Morocco, and his semi-independent "empire" gave the French no trouble. He was even willing to use his army to help the French defeat other Berber groups. For many years he was a corner-stone of French power in Morocco. More about him later.

While Lyautey was still whipping French Morocco

into shape, the Spaniards were having their own difficulties in Spanish Morocco. Their chief problem was a group of Berber tribes living in the hills of the Rif, an almost impenetrable region behind Tetuán, the Spanish Moroccan capital. In the 1920's a great chieftain of those tribes, a man named Abdel Krim, roused his people to a savage revolt that became a full-scale war. And the Spaniards were losing this war until the French came to their aid. Even then, with aeroplanes and the most modern weapons, the French and Spanish forces had a hard time crushing the ill-armed tribesmen of the Rif. In the end Abdel Krim was exiled, but the Spaniards were so fearful of further uprisings that they maintained military garrisons in practically every village and mountain settlement in their territory.

Lyautey left his post in 1926. By that time French Morocco—a "feudal slum" thirteen years before— had made great strides toward becoming a modern and united country. And much of the work he started continued under the various Residents General who followed him.

This new French "face" of Morocco showed itself in many ways. I have mentioned that the new French settlers—colons—became unpopular. But, on the credit side, they worked hard, cultivated land that had never been cultivated before and increased the yield on land that had always been called poor. They brought with them modern ideas of farming, good machinery, chemicals, seed and livestock. It was chiefly by their efforts that the country's wheat acreage eventually increased ten times, its number of date trees five times, its olive trees forty times.

When Lyautey arrived in 1912 the country didn't have a single bridge or an inch of railway line. Its roads were miserable beyond description, where they existed at all. But French enterprise built about seven thousand miles of highways, eleven hundred miles of railroad lines, eight modern ports, ninety-eight airfields and landing strips, and dams which provided water for irrigation and water power for electricity.

Industrialization made great strides too, to the point where more than two hundred thousand Moroccans were working in modern factories. The French also probed the Atlas for new mineral wealth, and extended mining operations.

Their record in public health was even more impressive. In 1912 the country had exactly one hospital, a mental institution where patients wore iron collars and were chained together night and day. The French, from 1912 to 1955, built something like five hundred hospitals, and more than a million Moroccans were given free medical examinations every year. Malaria was reduced. Old epidemic scourges like smallpox, plague and typhus were wiped out entirely.

Of course the public-health programme, and some of the other improvements made in Morocco, cost France a great deal of money. The French government had to contribute millions of francs every year to the Moroccan budget. But France did very well out of its protectorate. Frenchmen received the bulk of the profits from the new Moroccan industries and commercial ventures, because they controlled 80 per cent of them. Three hundred thousand colons, who would otherwise have been crowded into France herself, found living space and opportunity in Morocco. And as "protector" of Morocco, France had added to her prestige in the world.

As for the Moroccans themselves, some felt grateful to the French for uniting their country and setting it toward progress, as was natural. Arabs who had struggled all their lives to scratch a living out of tiny patches of arid soil, for example, were glad to be earning steady wages in a French-owned factory.

But after a time some Arabs came to realize that their wages were very low, compared to the profits being made by a French factory owner. They also began to realize that they—and probably their sons too—would never win better-paid jobs, because they would never get the opportunity to train themselves for anything but the lowest class of work. The Arabs began to resent all this. And, even more strongly, they resented political dominance and the French attitude expressed in that insulting phrase, "dirty Arabs."

Gradually, more and more Arabs became convinced that Moroccans would be better off if they had more say in their own affairs. Some of them went so far as to suggest that Morocco ought to get rid of her French overlords entirely. Those men became Morocco's first outspoken nationalists.

The urge toward independence developed slowly in Morocco, at least until the outbreak of the Second World War. But a few nationalist-minded

Algiers: Village children play after school

Morocco: A family return home from market

1,500 years ago this was the great Byzantine city of Sbeitla, in modern Tunisia

The great mosque at Kairouan in Tunisia, founded in the 7th century as the seat of Moslem learning

Arabs were active as early as 1927, when a new sultan came to the throne. This same man, after many ups and downs, was still Sultan when Morocco became an independent nation twenty-nine years later. This is why the history of those years can best be told by reference to the strange story of Sidi Mohammed Ben Youssef, better known outside his own country as Sultan Mohammed the Fifth, or simply as Mohammed V.

SULTAN MOHAMMED V

Mohammed V was enthroned when he was only seventeen years old. The Ulema of Fez named him —instead of naming one of his two elder brothers, for example—because he was the man the French wanted. The French thought he was too young to have any ideas of his own, and could be moulded into just the kind of docile puppet-sultan they liked.

For quite a while it seemed as if the French had made a good choice, from their own point of view. Mohammed V meekly signed all the *dahirs*—laws— which the Resident General presented to him. The only thing he seemed to care much about was enjoying himself, and spending enormous amounts of money.

He certainly had plenty to spend. His salary alone was £300,000 a year, and in addition to this he received a great deal of money from other sources. Whenever he appointed a pasha or a caid, for example, according to the ancient right of sultans, he

3

was paid handsomely for the appointment—because pashas and caids had to pay high sums for their posts. Each pasha also gave the Sultan a large gift, called a *heydia*, three times a year, and a single *heydia* might amount to thousands of pounds. The Sultan was also the head of Morocco's judicial system—a sort of one-man supreme court which made decisions in law cases involving business contracts, property and similar matters. And "buying" justice from the Sultan was an old, old Moroccan custom.

Sultan Mohammed V was therefore a very rich man while he was still quite young. Eventually he was said to be worth more than three million pounds.

Of course it cost him a good deal to keep up his royal position. He had to maintain about sixty palaces, hundreds—even thousands—of servants, and all the hangers-on who, by Islamic tradition, could never be turned away from the Sultan's door. He had two wives and at least forty or fifty concubines, the semi-legal wives permitted by Islamic tradition. But even with all these expenses he was able to spend a good deal of money on himself—for instance by collecting automobiles almost as an ordinary man might collect neckties.

Strangely enough, the one car the Sultan preferred to drive himself was a pint-sized Renault. He also liked to build things with his own hands, and to run a bulldozer. And this pudgy but athletic man played good tennis, almost of tournament quality—and one of his favourite partners was a cook from the royal kitchens.

But if the French noticed these remarkably democratic streaks in Mohammed's nature, they didn't take them seriously. In their eyes Mohammed V was a very satisfactory puppet indeed—that is, for a time.

During the years just before the Second World War the French realized that a handful of educated Arabs were talking about eventual freedom for Morocco. The French authorities promptly exiled the ringleaders of the various scattered little groups, but otherwise paid them little attention. They were confident that, with the help of the Sultan, they could always put down any such feeble expressions of nationalism.

Then in 1939, with the beginning of the war, things began to change fast and violently. Nazi Germany quickly conquered France, and set up a puppet French government at Vichy which extended its control to French North Africa. In 1942 the Americans landed at Casablanca, and for many months fighting took place all up and down the southern Mediterranean coast. Not until the Allies eventually defeated the Nazis could the true government of France once more take control of its North African territories.

It became immediately clear, then, that the French prestige in Morocco had been seriously damaged. The Moroccans had watched France collapse under the Nazi attack, and now they no longer regarded their "protector" as a strong power. The small Moroccan nationalist groups, hitherto weak, merged into a single independence party, the Istiqlal, which dared to speak up boldly to the French authorities.

Another factor which—according to the French —damaged their prestige in the country was this: when President Franklin Delano Roosevelt attended the famous Casablanca Conference of the Allied powers in 1943, he invited Sultan Mohammed V to dinner. And the Sultan accepted the invitation.

Incredible as it sounds, this was the first time since 1912 that any Sultan had ever seen a foreign dignitary except under the eye of French advisers, standing close by to keep an eye on him. The reason for the presence of those advisers was, of course, that since 1912 France had taken full charge of all Morocco's foreign relations, and the French didn't want the Sultan to exceed his authority. When the Moroccan Sultan met alone with the President of the United States, it was therefore an unprecedented event.

What the two men talked about has never been definitely known. But the French claim that President Roosevelt told the Sultan that Morocco should in time become independent of France—and repeated the advice again in a letter he wrote to Mohammed V from America.

Another thing happened not long afterward which gave strong encouragement to Moroccan nationalists. This was the founding of the United Nations in 1945. The charter written by its members stated that they believed in "equal rights and self-determination of peoples." And among the charter members of the organization were Egypt, Saudi Arabia, Syria and other Arab nations. Together they formed the nucleus of the future Arab bloc, bound together to promote the interests of all Arab countries—to work, in other words, toward "self-determination" for Arab peoples.

At about this time the Sultan seemed to "go sour," as the French expressed it. To their great amazement, he stopped being a man who jumped obediently whenever the Resident General pulled the strings. Mohammed V didn't become an aggressive nationalist. But he did make it clear that he wanted a more satisfactory partnership with France. He said he looked forward to eventual Moroccan independence, but on terms that would be fair to France and on some future date that he hoped France would name.

The Sultan's new stand seemed reasonable to many liberal-minded Frenchmen. But it horrified a good many others, and they immediately took the position which the French government clung to so stubbornly in the years that followed. The position was more or less that France refused to make any compromise at all with Morocco, and that it would maintain control of Morocco by military strength, if necessary.

The colons living in Morocco supported this extremist stand. So did bankers and industrialists who had investments there. So did many Berber pashas and caids, who scorned—almost more than the French did—what they called the Arab nationalist "riffraff." These groups all came to identify Mohammed V with the nationalists, simply because he had shown some independence of spirit. In their eyes the Sultan had suddenly become as dangerous as the most revolutionary member of the Istiqlal, Morocco's growing independence party.

THE ISTIQLAL

By 1950 the Istiqlal had become a powerful influence in Morocco. Its membership was largely Arab, and its greatest strength lay in the cities and towns, especially among workers. It was just beginning to win some support in the Berber regions. Naturally that old Berber chieftain, El Glaoui, staunch friend of the French, was strongly opposed to all it stood for.

Exactly what the Istiqlal did stand for was not easy to explain. Its members were of all shades of opinion—from those who sought mild reforms in the French administration to extremists who sought complete freedom from France. If France had listened to some of the moderates at the beginning, things might have turned out differently. But the French authorities, clinging to their no-compromise attitude, never even recognized the Istiqlal as a lawful political party. And this caused resentment against them, even among Moroccans who had never resented France before.

The French authorities did, however, give recognition of a grim sort—in the form of imprisonment or exile—to some of the Istiqlal's leaders. This is why Morocco's fight for freedom had to be directed largely from other countries, by men who had been forced to leave their homeland.

Two of those exiled leaders—Allal el Fassi and Hadj Ahmed Belafrej—were chiefly responsible for keeping the Istiqlal's programme alive, and for bringing it to the attention of the rest of the world, especially through the United Nations.

Allal el Fassi, a teacher by profession, was regarded by the French as the more dangerous of the two men. Exiled even before the Second World War, he had found a haven in Cairo, and warm encouragement from the Egyptians and from other Arab nations.

The other leader, Hadj Ahmed Belafrej, was more moderate than El Fassi. He wanted independence for his country, but he was not a violent extremist. He dreamed of a free Morocco that would live in close co-operation with the country that had "protected" her since 1912.

But while Belafrej was a student in France in 1928 —like many other North African political leaders, he had a good French education—he formed an Association of North African Moslem Students. This sort of activity alarmed the French so much that they exiled Belafrej too before the war started. When he returned home, and became secretary-general of the Istiqlal, the French exiled him again, this time to Corsica. A few years later he was at large once more, shuttling between Madrid and New York, the head-quarters of the Moroccan nationalists who were trying to air their grievances before the United Nations.

The French made blunder after blunder—so at least most people thought. And the Istiqlal drew up a long list of grievances against France. Summed up, the major ones were these:

1. Moroccans had no voice at all in the governing of their country.
2. Moroccans had no civil liberties. They could be arrested for almost anything—for gathering to hear a speaker, for going from one city to another without official permission, for reading an Istiqlal pamphlet—

and held in jail for as long as the French wished, without even being charged with any crime.

3. Out of forty-five thousand government employees, only sixty were Moroccans. The rest were French. And those sixty Moroccans had the lowest positions of all— as doormen, cleaners or menial clerks. This meant that Moroccans had no chance to learn how to run a government—and gave the French the chance to claim that Moroccans couldn't possibly manage their own affairs.

4. All French children in Morocco went to school, but only one-tenth of Morocco's two million native children had the opportunity to get an education. In the whole country only about fifteen thousand Moroccan boys were managing to get as far as secondary school, and only three hundred and fifty to a university.

5. The Moroccans had to support an army of about fifty thousand French troops—soldiers often used to break up or subdue their own nationalist activities.

6. Five thousand of the wealthier colons owned about one-tenth of all the arable land in the country. Thousands of other colons owned a great deal of the rest of it. But hundreds of thousands of Moroccans owned no land at all.

7. The French also controlled most of Morocco's natural resources, including her abundance of iron, coal, manganese, lead, zinc, copper and cobalt, plus her one operating oil field which they hoped would prove the first of many. The Moroccan government did own and control the country's phosphate resources (they are large enough to make it the second biggest phosphate producer in the world), but most other enterprises—including textile mills, shipyards, fishing fleets and hydroelectric stations—were in French hands. And the Moroccans employed by the French received very low wages.

8. The French didn't allow Moroccan workers to form their own trades unions, for fear that these unions would become nationalist centres. Moroccans could join only French trades unions.

9. The French gave no indication of ever intending to terminate their "protectorate" over Morocco at some future date, much less giving the country full freedom, as the United States had freed the Philippine Islands or as England freed India. So far as the Moroccans knew, France intended to maintain her control over Morocco for ever—unless the Moroccans themselves could break her power.

Gradually, from 1950 on, the nationalists' pleas for reforms turned into an active fight to break French rule. It took the form of strikes, sabotage, terrorist raids, riots and other "incidents," some of which were very violent.

One curious incident took place late in 1950, when El Glaoui left his stronghold at Marrakesh and called on the Sultan at Rabat. The old chieftain brought with him the seven million francs' tribute that was customary. But what he said to the Sultan that day was not customary. El Glaoui was one of the chieftains who most strongly accused the Sultan of dealings with "riffraff" nationalists, and on this occasion he blamed him outright for the unrest that had been stirring in some of his own Berber villages. He told Mohammed V that he ought to be ashamed of himself.

Mohammed V was furious. According to those who were present at the meeting he shouted, "Go, dog!" and showed El Glaoui the door. El Glaoui went—and without leaving the tribute the Sultan had expected.

Later came terrible riots in Casablanca and other cities. Nobody knows how many nationalists were shot down by French troops and police; the Moroccans say they lost 1,208 men. This tragic event gave the French an excuse to outlaw the Istiqlal, throw more than a thousand nationalists into jail and ship countless others to concentration camps in the desert.

Then, in August 1953, came a tremendous crisis. El Glaoui's warriors, armed with their ancient muskets, marched into the towns and surrounded the Sultan's palace in Rabat. The old chieftain had made this kind of dramatic show of force before, in attempting to get rid of his enemy the Sultan, but the French were hesitant to take the extreme step of actually ousting the Sultan from the throne. But this time the French Resident General took quick advantage of El Glaoui's move, and the authorities in Paris didn't interfere. First he surrounded the Sultan's palace with his own troops too, explaining that their purpose was to "protect" the besieged Sultan. Then—as France had done in 1912—he demanded a price for saving Mohammed V from his Berber subjects. The price was the Sultan's signature to new decrees that put the throne under stricter discipline than ever.

The Sultan had no choice. With the Istiqlal outlawed, and most of its powerful members in jail or in exile, he could expect no organized support if he refused. But the Sultan's capitulation was not enough for El Glaoui or the French. Before the curtain came down the old Berber chieftain succeeded in influencing the French to depose Mohammed V, and he was thrown off the throne. On August 20, 1953, French officials hustled the Sultan out of the country, first to Corsica and then to the distant island of Madagascar on the far side of the African continent.

The man who had never been a revolutionist himself, who had wanted only a fairer partnership between his country and France, was transformed by this event into a living symbol of Morocco's fight for freedom. And now the battle quickened.

THE NEXT ACT

On the very day after Mohammed V's departure, the French—with the meek approval of the Ulema of Fez—installed a new monarch on the Moroccan throne, a monarch of a very different kind. He was an old man, far too old, the French thought, ever to pick up modern ideas of nationalism. He was gentle and peaceable. He was El Glaoui's personal choice, and a relative of the veteran Berber chief. Like El Glaoui himself, he was devoted to the French. We will call him, for the sake of convenience, Mohammed VI. His full name was Sidi Mohammed Ben Moulay Arafa el Alaoui.

Sultan Mohammed VI lasted just a little over two years.

During that time the French talked a great deal about the reforms they planned to put into effect in Morocco—reforms which would give the people some say in their own government, and more freedom in their daily lives. The man who tried hardest to put those reforms into practice was a courageous and sensible human being, Pierre Mendès-France, who became prime minister of the French government in 1954.

When Mendès-France took office his country was suffering a disastrous defeat in Asia, where it had tried—and failed—to hold on to its colony of Indo-China by force of arms. Mendès-France was convinced that military might alone could not hold French North Africa any longer. So he suggested that France offer Morocco "home rule"—that is, control over her internal affairs—and leave only Morocco's defence and foreign relations in French hands, with close economic ties.

But all those groups who hated the Moroccan nationalists now turned their hatred on Mendès-France too. They screamed fiercely at the very idea of giving any power or privileges to the "dirty Arabs," and Mendès-France was forced to resign. The possibility of compromise, and of the talked-of reforms, was pretty much forgotten.

New fighters for Moroccan freedom seemed to spring up overnight, to replace those the French arrested. One of the chief targets of their anger was the elderly Sultan, who barely escaped assassination on two occasions. It steadily became more difficult for the French to keep any sort of order in Morocco. Shootings and bombings were incessant. Three long days of violent bloodletting, for example, marked the second anniversary of Mohammed V's exile. Villages were burned and looted, a valuable phosphate plant was destroyed and three hundred people were killed.

One of the most startling aspects of this grave riot

was the fact that so many Berbers took part in it. Until then the French had thought they could probably pacify Morocco in time by the old method of playing on Berber sympathy. This show of Berber violence proved that even El Glaoui could no longer keep all his tribesmen loyal to France.

Finally a new Resident General suggested a face-saving device. He recommended replacing the hated new Sultan with a regency council, and giving this body the right to work out a plan for Moroccan home rule.

But even with the scheme officially approved, and the Istiqlal members in exile showing their willingness to negotiate on the terms that had been offered, nothing definite happened. Killings and terrorist raids occurred daily, and the French shilly-shallied. They were still hoping that the formidable old warrior, El Glaoui, would be influential enough to pacify the country, end the crisis, and make French rule safe.

Then suddenly El Glaoui did act—but in a most unexpected way. On October 25, 1955, the eighty-four-year-old Berber chieftain asked the French to restore the exiled Mohammed V to the Moroccan throne. In other words he was bringing back his own chief enemy to the throne—the man he himself had helped to depose.

This sensational and abrupt about-face, made without warning, was a stunning blow to France. The gaunt old Berber was apparently admitting, publicly, that the nationalists were now too strong to be put down by the combined French-Berber forces. So nationalism won. Now it was too late to set up the regency council that had been discussed for so long, too late even to hope that the Moroccans would be satisfied with mere home rule, or with anything less than complete independence.

Grimly the French took the first swallow of what they now knew would be a long dose of bitter medicine. They sent a 'plane to Madagascar to bring the exiled Sultan home. A dramatic confrontation followed.

On November 9, 1955, El Glaoui ceremoniously called on Sultan Mohammed V, now restored to his throne, and got down on his knees to crawl the length of the room and kiss the hem of the monarch's robe. And this was the man whom he, El Glaoui, had forced into exile only two years before!

Photographers' flash bulbs popped as the once-proud warrior humiliated himself and mumbled, "I am a slave at the feet of your Majesty."

"Do not speak to me any more of the past," the Sultan replied. "What counts now is the future."

On March 2, 1956—forty-four years after Morocco accepted foreign "protection"—a new protocol was signed between France and the Sherifian Empire, which made Morocco an independent state. The following month Spain also recognized the triumph of the nationalists, and Spanish Morocco became a part of the new Morocco. Then a series of negotiations handled by Morocco's new foreign minister—he was Hadj Ahmed Belafrej, back home from New York after his exile—brought Tangier under Moroccan rule as well.

In November 1956, Morocco took its seat in the United Nations, her political independence established before the whole world.

WHAT LIES AHEAD FOR MOROCCO?

Moroccans are now learning, as Indians have learned in recent years, that independence is not an end, but only a beginning. When they took over the right to govern themselves, they also took over responsibility for the continued existence and the welfare of their country. The problems that face them—financial, political, educational, administrative—all have to be solved by Moroccans.

Of the many tasks that faced the Sultan and his government, the most important, perhaps, was the development of a new relationship between Morocco and France—an "interdependence," as it has been called, which will be of mutual benefit to both countries.

After the bitter struggle Moroccans waged for their freedom, it may seem strange that any of them should now want to build up close ties with France. But the fact is that unless Morocco can continue to receive various kinds of French aid, her future is uncertain. Conversely, France is far too deeply involved in Morocco to be willing to pull out of the country entirely and write off as a loss all her investments there.

Morocco certainly needs economic help. Morocco is not a particularly poor country, either in agricultural production or in natural resources. But Moroccans themselves don't have the wealth to buy up the mines, industries and agricultural enterprises now largely owned by French interests. And Moroccans don't yet have the technical skill to run such enterprises even if they did own them. So, if

Morocco got rid of the French entirely, she would lose almost as much by the process as the French themselves.

In such matters as running the country, building schools, developing housing projects and expanding public health, Morocco is also dependent on French help. Thousands of Frenchmen are still employed by Morocco in the everyday administration of the government. They may irritate the Moroccan nationalists, but the country can't yet get along without them. This too, of course, strengthens the French hand in talks between the two countries.

The confused political picture inside newly independent Morocco further complicates her relations with France. Morocco is pretty well united in its loyalty to Mohammed V, but is split into hostile groups on almost every other subject. There is the hard core of the old ruling class—the pashas and caids—who still think longingly of the good old days when their feudal way of life was unchanged. There are the colons, some of them still hopeful of reviving the old Arab-Berber animosity, so that France could take the country over again with the excuse of maintaining peace. There is the Istiqlal, largest and most important of Morocco's political parties, whose leaders are demanding that the tremendous holdings of the pashas and caids be taken over and distributed among Morocco's poor landless farmers.

Even the Istiqlal is divided within itself. There are moderates who want to continue working with France. There are extremists who are not only anti-French, but against anything and everything of the Western world. These extremists pin their hopes on the growing power of the Arab bloc, and have even joined the anti-Israel campaign which is the rallying cry of the Arab states of the Middle East. If they cause a mass emigration of Jews from Morocco, the country would suffer a heavy loss of skilled manpower. This is one reason why the Sultan quickly promised fair treatment to all Jews who remained in independent Morocco.

As for Mohammed V himself, he is trying to steer a middle course. He has proved himself willing to work with France, but he hopes France will some day give up all her African colonies. He clearly favours closer ties between Morocco and the United States. He also wants to improve the wages and living conditions of the great mass of Moroccan farmers and workers. But, because he is after all a king, and thus a representative of the ruling class, he cannot wholly support the drastic schemes for reform that would cut down the landholdings of Morocco's wealthy aristocrats.

But also Mohammed V is trying to make the country more democratic. He doesn't want to be an absolute monarch any longer, preferring, he says, to be the "constitutional sovereign of a modern democracy." He has even said that he prefers to be called a king, rather than by the traditional title of sultan. He has broken the old tradition of the Ulema by naming his eldest son as heir to the throne. He has approved the establishment of a parliament that represents all shades of Moroccan political opinion, and has repeated his firm belief that Morocco must have a popularly elected government and a constitution that guarantees equality and justice for all Moroccans. But it will be years before all Moroccans are ready to understand and use the ballot. Educating the people for full political independence will take a long, long time.

As for El Glaoui, he is dead. The old Berber warrior passed away peacefully in his sleep late in 1956.

5

More About Morocco
—Its Sights and Cities

RABAT, the capital of Morocco, has one chief business: government. In its European quarter stand the modest but impressive buildings—erected under the eye of Lyautey himself—that once housed a French Resident General and his staff. Here the wide streets, bordered by villas behind brightly flowering shrubbery, have the general flavour of Canberra, another city designed to be a nation's capital.

Not far from the French-built Residency stands the nation's Imperial Palace. Like most Moroccan palaces it is shabby and unsubstantial-looking on the outside. But its interior is marked by a peculiarly oriental grandeur and magnificence, full of clashing colours. The gigantic unpaved court that faces it is also typical of Moroccan royal architecture. Known as a *mechouar*, it is used as a parade ground and a setting for the ceremonies of homage which tribes and their chieftains still perform before the King.

Rabat's population, about 160,000, is a hodge-podge of mountain tribesmen, Arabs in dingy robes, smartly dressed French women, heavily veiled Moslem women and American GI's from nearby bases.

Rabat and her pretty little sister city, Salé—home port of the dreaded "Sally Rovers" when piracy was Morocco's most important industry—are connected by a bridge across the Bou Regreg River. But an old saying has it that the two cities will never be friends "until the sands become raisins and the river milk." Unlike Rabat, Salé has remained a purely Arab community, and is a kind of unofficial headquarters for the more progressive-minded Moroccan intellectuals.

ROMANTIC FEZ

Fez is one of the most romantic cities in the world. It is almost sinister in its atmosphere of closedness and secrecy, with twisting alleys and buildings in sombre shades of grey, black and white. Lying inland, in a secluded green valley, abundantly watered by two streams, it is the intellectual, spiritual and artistic capital of Morocco.

Except in the new part of Fez, built after the French came, the streets are mostly too narrow for automobiles, or even for bicycles. Hemmed in between garden and house walls, they are mere corridors, sometimes stairways, made of dirt or cobbles and protected from the sun by trellises, mats and screens.

The sook, or market, is the most colourful I ever saw. Here in an enclosed and limited space—a city within a city—a purchaser may buy almost anything from DDT to flasks of perfume, from live goats to *majoun*, a candied form of the narcotic hashish. All of Morocco's handicraft products can be purchased here—rugs, pottery, embroidery and copperwork, and the world-famous morocco leather. This city has been an important trade centre for centuries, and once it boasted two hundred caravanserais, or hotels, each with fifty to a hundred rooms.

The university attached to the great Kairouyine mosque—Fez has hundreds of mosques—is one of the best known in the Islamic world. Its students huddle in cold cells, get a loaf of bread a day and learn by listening hour after hour to ancient sages. Most of them wear the brimless red felt hat, with its dangling tassel, which is called a fez because it was once the exclusive speciality of this city. Here the berries grew that were used to dye it a characteristic shade of bright maroon.

In addition to its Moslem flavour, Fez has a strong Spanish strain. Its population, about two hundred thousand, includes the descendants of eight thousand Spanish families that settled here in medieval times. And a Jewish influence, which also came from Spain, is noticeable too. In general, the people are the palest I saw anywhere in North Africa—even paler than most Berber hillsmen.

Surrounded by terraced vineyards and orchards, Fez is a rich community, a city of wealthy merchants and upper-middle-class Arabs. It is also an extremely sophisticated city, and Fezis look down on the Berbers to the south as illiterate ruffians. It is full of men of learning. But Fez also has its quota of poor workers, labouring for miserable wages under near-feudal conditions, and its quota of blind and maimed beggars too. At the railway station, waiting for a train after midnight, I saw what seemed to be a disorderly heap of mail sacks piled on each other. They were poor Arabs, sleeping in their ragged burnooses.

CASABLANCA, NORTH AFRICAN METROPOLIS

If Rabat is Morocco's Canberra, Casablanca is certainly its Sydney. This busy, lively, fast-growing port, fifty-six miles south of Rabat on the Atlantic, is the commercial, financial and industrial heart of the nation. Its population, now numbering about eight hundred thousand, is increasing rapidly. Casablanca is the largest city in Morocco, and one of the four or five largest in all Africa.

Casablanca was nothing but a huddle of fishermen's huts several decades ago, but today it resembles Rio de Janeiro or, perhaps, Miami. Its white buildings, bright with glass and hung with balconies in the most modern manner, present a glittering façade to the Atlantic. Here the visitor can find anything he might expect in a booming new city anywhere—luxurious hotels, Parisian restaurants, wide boulevards humming with sleek cars, beautiful shops and what is certainly one of the world's largest swimming pools. It is more than a quarter of a mile long!

Casablanca has a fairly typical old medina—native quarter—tucked away near the waterfront. It has a new medina too, French-designed and with good sanitation. Casablanca also has a third native quarter, and this one is a squalid collection of miserable huts built largely out of five-gallon petrol cans hammered flat. The French word for can, *bidon*, gives it its name, Bidonville. Other Moroccan cities have Bidonvilles too, caused by the rapidly expanding population and housing shortage. The one in Casablanca is noteworthy because it is the largest and most sordid. Americans who visit it are usually reminded of the shantyvilles that sprang up during the years of economic depression on the edges of their big cities.

THE AMERICAN BASES

Casablanca is a good starting point for a round of visits to Morocco's five American bases (not counting the headquarters of the Fifth Air Division at Rabat). Most of them are located close to the coast and either north or south of this glistening metropolis.

These bases were set up in 1951, when American soldiers were fighting in Korea and there was widespread fear of a general war between the United States and the Soviet Union. Building them constituted the biggest job ever undertaken by the U.S.

Army Engineers, and the largest American military project abroad since the Second World War. Civilian contractors helped. The work was done in such a hurry that it was botched in some respects, and gave rise to charges of waste, graft and inefficiency.

On the way from Casablanca to Marrakesh I visited the base at Nouasseur, which is the chief supply and repair depot for the whole group. Nouasseur is not merely an airfield, one of the largest in the world; it is a city, rough at the edges but a real city just the same. About six thousand Moroccan families had to be displaced to make room for it, and the work cost several hundred million dollars.

The base has six hundred thousand square feet of building space just for machine shops and the like, and twenty-three petrol pits, each one capable of pumping fuel into an aircraft at the rate of six hundred gallons a minute. But what impressed me most was the warehouse. I never realized before what a lot of things the American taxpayer's money goes for. Here were huge quantities of practically everything that an army, or a city, might conceivably need in a long war, from canned meat to nuts and bolts. I don't suppose it can be possible, but I think I saw ten thousand brooms.

A little farther along the same road I stopped briefly at another one of the bases, Ben Guerir, with a runway that is longer than New York's Central Park. Built of two layers of macadam, on solid rock, it looks like a grey moon flattened out.

MARRAKESH, THE "CITY OF MOROCCO"

Marrakesh, with a population of about 240,000, is the biggest city in Morocco after Casablanca. It was the largest city in the country before Casablanca recently mushroomed to its present size. And it is very, very old.

Since its founding in 1062 Marrakesh has been a great market town for the tribes of the northwestern Sahara. Caravans crossed this spot long before the city itself was here. In fact the city's name is said to come from a Berber phrase which means "Go quickly!"—a phrase often spoken in this neighbour-hood because bandits were common here and travellers were always in haste to pass through to a safer area. Marrakesh grew lustily. Soon it was so large and important that Europeans began to use its name for the whole surrounding territory. And Marrakesh, as the Europeans spoke it, became "Morocco."

Marrakesh is often called the "red city," and the red sands of the Sahara lap at its feet. But a semi-circle of snow-capped mountains rises behind it, and the city itself is like a garden. Here are orange trees and cypresses, bougainvillaea and hibiscus, hedges boiling with roses and date palms clear and sharp against the sky. Marrakesh is a sister city to Seville, Spain. The same architect helped design many of the chief buildings of both.

Nevertheless Marrakesh as a whole gives a totally African impression. Its pulse is that of Saharan Africa at its most intense. The streets are much less tortuous, less cramped, than in Fez. Even the market seems relatively open, and one gets an occasional glimpse of brilliant sky through lattices or screens.

This market is a place of primitive, lively, savage colours. Here are sienna-tinted Tuareg in indigo veils, and Senegalese from below the Sahara, as black as blindness. There are skins of every possible shade—mahogany, bronze, chocolate, beige, russet, tar paper. I saw a prancing white stallion up for sale and, not far away, heaps of leather baboo-shes, or slippers, in vivid gold and blue. The dye sellers sit behind radiant pools of ultramarine and scarlet.

This seething, multicoloured market bursts out of its bounds and spews into an open space, the size of half a dozen American city blocks, called the Djemma el Fna, or Place of the Dead. This is one of the supreme sights of Africa, or anywhere else. It is not a place of death at all, but of life—teeming life. It is a combination of market, parade ground and place of entertainment—a sort of African Coney Island. One curious point is that, even in the heat of day, the countrymen who crowd into it are huddled into heavy clothes. This is because they cannot afford a room at a fondouk, or inn, and have no place to leave extra garments. They wear every-thing they own, and bring their animals along, too.

The best time to visit the Place of the Dead is at dusk. Then small flares light up each patch of enter-tainers—snake charmers, magicians with live doves, fire-eaters, storytellers enthralling rapt listeners. One sight not easily forgotten is the chain of blind beggars that cuts its way through the throbbing crowds, holding itself together by clasped hands.

DINNER WITH THE PASHA

The Pasha of Marrakesh, El Glaoui, lived in this city until his death in 1956. In fact, Marrakesh was his capital. I was fortunate enough to meet the Lord of the Atlas, as the powerful old chieftain was often called, before he died. I was even more fortunate in being invited, with several other guests, to a *diffa* or banquet in his rambling yellowish palace. It was an occasion I will always remember.

When we arrived at the palace we were met by twenty bearded retainers, or servants, looking like a line of owls. They led us to a small room with maroon-striped settees, green curtains and a brilliant yellow carpet. Moslems love discordant colours. A cold wind whipped through the door and windows, which are usually kept open at ceremonies of this kind, no matter how chilly it may be outside. Birds sometimes fly in and out of the windows during a meal.

El Glaoui, who had been sitting alone on a hassock, rose to greet us. He wore Arab dress, a *djellaba*, but beneath it he was wearing an American-style shirt and a red tie. And he had checkered socks on his slippered feet. After greeting his guests he led us across a courtyard filled with orange trees to another section of the palace where an American-style cocktail bar was in operation. Of course neither the Glaoui nor his Arab guests drank any alcoholic beverages, but he had no objection to serving such drinks to non-Moslems.

Finally dinner was announced, by a servant who entered abruptly and twitched the Glaoui's elbow in the peculiar informal manner of Moroccan servants. We all went outdoors again, crossed another courtyard and entered a room big enough to seat two hundred. The chief colours here were pink, lettuce-green and purple. The Pasha sat down on a divan and invited us to sit around him.

When it comes to food, nothing is more fascinating than an Arab *diffa*, but a guest is at a disadvantage if he doesn't know ahead of time more or less what to expect. Here are a few of the things that it is helpful to know:

Guests at a *diffa* are seated on cushions or low divans. The large white napkin laid over each guest's knees may be used, but not too conspicuously, to clean the lips, but not the fingers.

Except in special cases there are no knives, forks, spoons, plates or other implements. The tablecloth is laid on the floor, directly in front of the diners, to catch crumbs. Guests help themselves, with their fingers, from central platters or casseroles.

Bread, which is served in large soft chunks, may be eaten with the left hand. Otherwise only the right hand is supposed to touch food, and only the thumb and first two fingers of that hand should be used. The fingers are not supposed to touch the lips—the food is tossed into the mouth. This is simple enough with some kinds of food—but try to pick up a blazing hot fried egg with three fingers and get it into your mouth without touching your lips, or spilling!

A servant arrives with a pitcher and pours water into a bowl, over the hands of each guest, at the beginning and end of the meal.

As each course is finished, the dish is removed to a different part of the house where the women are waiting. When the wives and concubines have had their share it goes in turn to male servants, female servants and finally to hangers-on at the gate.

This is what we ate at the banquet in El Glaoui's palace, after the traditional serving of sweet, sticky mint tea:

First a pale green soup composed of almonds, peas and bits of white fish. The soup was a concession to the Westerners among the guests. We were even given plates and spoons.

Second a whole roast lamb, known as a *mechoui*, a standard course at any elaborate *diffa*. With great dexterity the Glaoui broke into the hot crackling skin to find specially tender morsels which he passed on with his fingers to his guests. Nobody at an Arabian *diffa* tears off big chunks of flesh. People eat slivers and delicate strips, more as if they were merely tasting than as if they were satisfying hunger. And this is a wise precaution, because there is so much to eat at a *diffa* that barely tasting each course is enough.

Third we had a *pastilla*, the pride of a good Moroccan cook. This is a pie which takes almost two full days to prepare. The one we had that day was almost three feet in diameter, with a wonderfully fine flaky crust, underneath which we found shrimp, tripe, sweetbreads, olives, liver, mussels and fried eggs.

After this we had four more main courses. First squabs, then roast chickens stuffed with olives, then two different kinds of lamb. Following this we were served a dish of strangely shaped pretzels, seasoned with molasses, a sweet interlude to refresh our already tired appetites for what was to come.

Couscous was next. This is the basic food of Morocco for rich and poor alike. Its main ingredient is the wheat cereal called semolina. The kernels are cooked until they are dry and served heaped high on a platter. Inside the towering mound of grain there may be anything from grapes to chunks of mutton. The couscous we had at the Pasha's palace contained turnips, carrots and hazelnuts.

Couscous, like rice in Japan, is always served toward the end of the meal so that you can fill up if you are still hungry. To take too much is bad manners; it implies that you weren't given enough food before. The cooked grain is very hard to manage with the fingers, since it is almost as dry as sand. The Glaoui was one of the world's foremost makers of couscous balls. We watched him, fascinated, as he picked up a clump of the blistering hot grain with thumb and two fingers, and let it fall into the palm of his hand. Then, without letting the fingers touch the grain again, he tossed it gently in the hollow of his palm until by some miracle it formed a ball. With a quick motion he popped the ball of couscous into his mouth, catching it on the fly. It was like watching a man make and eat golf balls with one hand.

At last came a cake made of frozen figs and tangerines. Then the Pasha picked up his napkin, and with a flourish dropped it on the tablecloth. This is the conventional gesture to indicate that a meal is over.

INTO THE KASBAH COUNTRY

After leaving Marrakesh I crossed the High Atlas by car and descended into the wild stubborn terrain beyond. There for the first time, I began to get a direct intimate view of primitive Morocco. This was nothing like the northern part of the country with its orderly expanses of French-owned farm land, vineyards and orchards. Nor was it like the poorer and smaller Berber farms, with their tiny fields and crude implements. This was the beginning of the *kasbah* country—the real feudal Morocco.

The word *kasbah*, though often used for the native quarter of a city, really means a stronghold, or a castle. A *kasbah*—that is, a castle—is made of dried mud and rises up like a medieval fortress, except that its towers are square instead of round. Many of these castles date back to the time of the Arab conquest of Morocco, and have changed very little since then. Richard the Lion-Hearted would have loved them, and so would Metro-Goldwyn-Mayer.

One of the roads I took was solid with crumbling *kasbahs*, but on another they were spaced out a mile or so apart. Some are deserted, but some still contain family groups of, say, a hundred people each, living under their chief in pretty much the same way their ancestors did—except that the old tribal wars are now a thing of the past.

As I left the Atlas behind, and approached the Sahara, I found myself driving over earth that was positively crimson. The people here are strikingly different from those in the mountain areas. Some children wore topknots as the Chinese do, because

—they said—a pigtail makes it easier for Mohammed to pick them up and carry them aloft to heaven.

This was primitive feudal Morocco at its oldest,
but even here the old and the new clashed. One
minute I passed a stately camel caravan, the next
minute a convoy of trucks loaded with manganese.
The big item on sale in one village market was
donkey dung for fuel, but that town also had a shiny
new Texaco station on one side of its square and a
Mobiloil petrol pump on the other.

TANGIER

Tangier is an oddity among cities. Since it became
an international zone, early in this century, its residents have paid no income tax, no sales tax, no gift
tax and no inheritance tax. Rich Britons, whose es-
tates would be almost wiped out by English death
duties, can leave big fortunes intact if they establish
residence in Tangier. And any person with a valid
passport can become a legal resident of Tangier
simply by moving there.

Tangier's banking laws are so lax that practically
anybody can open or run a bank whether or not he
has any real capital. Similarly anybody can form a
corporation and be almost totally exempt from the
usual rules designed to protect stockholders. There
are no currency-exchange restrictions whatever. You
can walk down a street in Tangier and buy the
money of a dozen different countries—or sell it just
as easily. For anyone inclined to be a crook, a spy,

'Nowhere in North Africa do men live in more primitive conditions.' Adobe houses for Tunisians, consisting of one room, one door, and no windows, the outside 'stairs' being toeholds cut into the mud

The inside of a troglodyte dwelling place inhabited by the Arabs of
Southern Tunisia

a smuggler, a tax-dodger, a gold hoarder, a money speculator or a shady financier, Tangier offers a setting almost too perfect to be believed.

A resident of Tangier is called a Tangerine. The name is the same as that of the well-known fruit. But it is uncertain whether Tangier was named for the fruit, or vice versa. In Tangier tangerines (the fruit) are called "mandarins." Anyway, there are some one hundred and seventy thousand Tangerines in the city—about one hundred and ten thousand native Moroccans and sixty thousand foreigners. Spaniards form the largest of the foreign communities. Tangier also has about twenty thousand Jews, some of very ancient stock, some that came from Spain in medieval times, and some who fled twentieth-century Nazi persecution.

These days most foreign Tangerines are badly worried. As an American newspaper headlined it, "Tangier Turmoil: Tiny Shadowy Land of Fiscal Freedom Has the Shakes."

What bothers the Tangerines is that they don't know how much longer they'll be allowed their tax-and-regulation-free existence now that Tangier is part of modern Morocco. No safeguards were written into the agreement that ended the former international control of the city. In fact, the eight foreign nations that once jointly ran Tangier simply renounced all their rights there, and left it to Mohammed V to determine what special privileges foreign citizens would enjoy.

The Moroccan government has stated that, for the present at least, Tangier's peculiar financial status would not be seriously disturbed. And it is

4

obvious that the Moroccan government, badly in
need of money, benefits handsomely from the foreign
capital that Tangier attracts. But Tangier's foreign
residents don't feel completely easy about the future.
Mohammed V can too easily change his mind, or
have it changed for him by a surge of pro-Arab or
anti-West sentiment among his people.

The primary interest of the United States in Tangier is the city's "radio power." It is one of the great
wireless crossroads of the world, partly because of
its location, but more because of its weather. Tangier
suffers very little natural radio interference, and
good transmission is generally possible twenty-four
hours a day, twelve months a year. With Tangier as
a relay point, practically every listening target in
Europe, Africa and the Middle East can be reached.
This is vitally important to American commercial
networks like RCA and Radio Mackay, which have
transmitters there, and also to the government-
operated Voice of America.

So far Morocco's government has agreed to allow
those three American radio installations to continue
their operations pending future negotiations. Morocco has already hinted, however, that she would
like to collect a tax of nearly a penny per word on all
the messages transmitted through Tangier by RCA
and Radio Mackay—a levy that would yield the
country about half a million dollars a year.

Tangier has always been a strict town for Moslems, and has become even stricter now that it is
part of independent Morocco. Most Moslem women
you see there are heavily muffled in white veils.
(Should you by chance see an unveiled native

woman, she is probably a peasant from the mountainous Rif, where women go unveiled.) Tangerine women are even forbidden to enter theatres. And banners strung across the streets carry the warning that Moslems of opposite sexes caught walking—or even talking—together, will be arrested unless they can prove they are married. Moslem men caught drinking anything stronger than tea or coffee are arrested and punished by a stiff fine and a term in jail. Women offenders draw the same penalties, except they they suffer the additional indignity of having their eyebrows and hair shaved off.

Whether this drive toward stricter enforcement of the Islamic code will increase or diminish, no one can say. In fact, no one can make any very definite guesses about the future of Tangier in general, any more than it is possible to make clear guesses about the future of Morocco as a whole. Its future depends on a great many things—the help the country may be able to obtain from other nations, the zeal with which its own people tackle the hard problems that face them, the easing of the tension and ill-will that exist throughout all North Africa and are especially strong between Arabs and colons here.

Moroccans fought successfully for their freedom. It is to be hoped that now they can forget the bitterness of that struggle, and direct all their efforts and energies toward the job of unifying, educating and developing their new nation.

THE UNITED STATES AND MOROCCO

Morocco's relations with the United States are important to her. Morocco is important to the U.S.A., too, although Moroccans say they haven't always acted as if they thought so.

During the period when the nationalists were fighting for independence, for example, the United States expressed a general sympathy with their aims. But when the Moroccan question came up for debate in the UN, the U.S. voted with France to block open discussion of the subject.

As a result the Moroccans quite naturally asked:

Why did the Americans support France, if they believe—as they say they do—in the right of people to self-government?

The truth was that the United States was caught in a trap at that time. As people who had fought for their own freedom, they had a natural sympathy for Morocco's hope to be free. But they had alliances with France; they would need her military aid in Europe if another war broke out there; they didn't want to do anything to hurt or weaken her. So the U.S. State Department tried to strike a balance between the two contrary points of view.

Now the situation is not so complicated, and the United States is committed to give Morocco some concrete economic help. Almost as soon as Moroccan independence was established, the U.S. government sent experts there to look over the field, to see what they could do in the way of assisting work projects and the like. One object is to help cut down

Moroccan unemployment, which has risen seriously in recent years.

Of course it is to America's interest to win and keep Moroccan friendship, and to give her aid she might otherwise seek from some anti-Western nation —from, say, the Soviet Union. And, obviously, the United States will not find it easy to operate their tremendous new air bases in Morocco smoothly without Moroccan consent and friendly co-operation.

Those bases were built while Morocco was still a protectorate, and arrangements for them were made with France—and only with France. The Sultan wasn't even officially informed that the bases were going to be built, and that Morocco would thus become a part of America's defence programme whether she liked it or not. In fact when the Sultan's eldest son, Prince Moulay Hassan, hopped into his car one day and drove out to visit one of the bases, the French were outraged. So now all countries must respect Moroccan sensitiveness about her sovereign rights.

There is also the matter of Morocco's long Atlantic coastline. By modern jet plane or guided missile Morocco is only a hop, skip and a jump from the Western hemisphere. And if Morocco should form an alliance with some anti-Western nation—because she cannot get the help she needs from the West— America might find a potential enemy directly across the ocean from her shores. Then the great bases in Morocco might conceivably be used against the U.S.

For the security of all the freedom-loving countries,

therefore, as well as for the sake of keeping Morocco a free nation, it is important to hold her on the democratic side of the world's political ledger. We shall be making a mistake if we don't help in her difficult battle against poverty, disease and ignorance.

6

Crisis and Tumult in Tunisia

THE new republic of Tunisia, smallest of our four
countries, is perhaps the most interesting of all.

It measures scarcely 125 miles from east to west,
and 500 miles from north to south, covering an area
about twice the size of Ireland. It occupies only
about one-thirty-sixth of North Africa, and half the
country is barren desert. Its 3,800,000 inhabitants
(240,000 of these are Europeans, mostly French, but
with sizeable Italian and Jewish colonies too) could
all be squeezed into the city of Chicago.

But Tunisia is as crowded with history as it is
with people. This little promontory, jutting toward
Europe at the midway point of the Mediterranean
coast, has played a lively part in North Africa's
past. Sometimes invaders who barely reached Morocco to the west, or Libya to the east, completely overran it. And Tunisia contains at least a
sample—is some cases a striking sample—of every
variety of North African geography: sandy seacoast,
forested mountains, fertile plains and desert dry as
sawdust.

Tunisia is, in other words, a kind of North-Africa-in-miniature, and for this reason alone it is noteworthy.

Each of the four quarters of this roughly rectangular little country has its own characteristics.

The northwest quarter is green and rich. Except during years of severe drought, it is greener and richer than any area in North Africa. Here are mountains cloaked with oak, rising almost straight out of the sea. Behind them are lower hills and plateaux, with ancient Phoenician and Roman ruins scattered everywhere like pebbles on a beach.

There are small deposits of iron in these hills, and sizable deposits of phosphate, valuable for fertilizers. Sheep graze on the plateaux, and nomads gather the white-plumed alfa grass. The dried grass is used for making ropes, nets, mats and other articles.

The adjoining northwest area also has mountains, hills and fertile plains. Here is concentrated Tunisia's immense wealth in olives. The country has twenty-five million olive trees; and the old story is that when a Tunisian picks up an olive, he says, "This is my gold." (Other important products are grain, wine and cork.)

This quarter also has great Roman ruins, as well as the ruins of North Africa's first metropolis, Carthage. Nearby is the former pirate stronghold, Tunis, now the nation's capital, and Bizerta, a famous naval base. Here, only about a hundred miles from Sicily, France built the big naval installation which she called the "key" to her European "house."

The two southern quarters are very different. The southeast section, behind its green strip of Mediterranean coastland, consists chiefly of a desert ridged into soft red hills. Among them, huddled in caves dug into the side of deep pits, are a few ancient Berber people whose ways seem not to have changed for thousands of years. These people are real cave dwellers—troglodytes, to use the scientific term. Nowhere in North Africa do men live in more primitive conditions. They make no pottery, they know very little about spinning, they seldom even build fires to cook their food.

The fourth, or southwest quarter, is mostly sandy desert, except for great stretches of salt marshes called chotts. A chott looks like a vast field of hard-packed snow crystals, but anybody who tries to cross it is risking his life. The soft quaking stuff under the glittering surface is as dangerous as quicksand.

Several delightful oases along the edge of the salt marshes are green with date palm trees. One brand of date grown here, called Deglet Nur, is said to be the best in all North Africa. Outside the oases the only inhabitants of this quarter are nomadic Arabs called Bedouin, who move their black tents with them as they wander about in search of pasturage for their flocks.

Tunisia is richer than Morocco in agriculture, but not so rich in minerals. She has some new industries, operating by means of electric power supplied by new dams. But forty thousand Tunisians—nearly as many as are employed by industry—still turn out the traditional handicraft products for which Morocco is also famous.

There are fewer European settlers here, in proportion to the whole population, than there are in

Algeria—though more than there are in Morocco. And these colons, as elsewhere in North Africa, once held almost all the civil service jobs, filled the bulk of the professional posts and owned a huge proportion of the large farms and profitable businesses.

WHY TUNISIA IS DIFFERENT

At first glance, then, this North-Africa-in-miniature seems to be pretty typical of North Africa as a whole.

Yet it isn't. As a nation Tunisia is strikingly different from its neighbours. It is more advanced, much closer in spirit to Europe and Western civilization in general, than Morocco or Libya.

Probably the chief reason for this is that Tunisia has no "hard core" of Berber population. Centuries ago most of the Berber tribes that lived here moved away, retreating from the waves of newcomers that occupied, one after the other, this busy crossroads of Mediterranean traffic. Today Tunisia's native population is almost totally Arab. And Arabs, as we have seen, are usually quicker to adjust to new ways, are more modern-minded, than most Berbers. Some Tunisian Arabs had become up-to-date landowners and businessmen even before the beginning of the French protectorate in 1881. They belonged to what the French call the *bourgeoisie* and what we call the middle class. They made up, in fact, the only really strong native middle class in all North Africa.

These middle-class Arabs appreciated the new roads the French built. They were grateful for improvements in public health made by the French. Most of them were soon speaking French, even to each other, and sending their sons to French schools and universities.

But they hated being ruled by the French, and they hoped to be strong enough some day to throw the French out. Shortly after the First World War they formed a political party called the Destour, or Constitution party. Its goal was the destruction of French power over their country.

A TUNISIAN HERO

In the late twenties there began to appear at Destour meetings an Arab lawyer named Habib Bourguiba, a short, slight young man with lively eyes and a gift for saying sober things in an exciting way. When he made a speech he could rouse his hearers to wild enthusiasm, but he himself never lost his head.

Independence for Tunisia was the dream of Bourguiba's life, but he didn't think it could be won by fighting on a battlefield. French power, he thought, didn't grow out of her guns and her military might. He believed it depended, instead, on the ignorance and meekness of the great majority of Tunisians— that is, the millions of Arabs who didn't belong to the comfortable middle class, who couldn't read or write, who laboured for starvation wages and who accepted their hard life without question because they believed it was Allah's will.

The Destour party, Bourguiba thought, should therefore not waste its energies quarrelling with France. It should set itself the more important job of educating and rousing the spirit of those down-trodden Tunisians, so that they would some day be ready for independence, and able to demand it.

France had built only a few schools in Tunisia, because—as in Morocco—it was to her advantage to keep most of the people uneducated. That's why Bourguiba thought a mass-education programme should be undertaken immediately.

He also wanted to convince the poorest and most miserable Arabs that their poverty and misery were not necessarily the will of Allah. He wanted to re-mind them that the French were not their masters by reason of some divine law, but that all men had the right to improve their own lives and destinies.

Bourguiba's ideas sounded like radical nonsense to those members of the Destour party who, like the French colons themselves, had nothing but scorn for the uneducated mass of Tunisians. But many Destourians were convinced that he was right. And when the more rigid tried to suppress him, he and his friends formed a new party called the Neo-Destour. (Neo means "new.") It developed into an organization very much like the Istiqlal of Morocco, but better grounded and more mature. Bourguiba remained its leader in the long struggle that fol-lowed, although more often than not he had to carry on his work from exile or from a prison cell.

Habib Bourguiba deliberately trained himself for

the job he was tackling. Born in the quiet little sea-side town of Monastir, in 1903, he was sent to Tunis at the age of five to be educated under the direction of his two older brothers. It was one of his own brothers, who was in charge of a hospital where Bourguiba spent several months recovering from a serious illness, who gave young Habib the ideas that affected his whole life.

This brother, Mohammed, believed intensely in the importance of human dignity. Anything that destroyed that dignity—whether it was a French overlord, or an ancient Moslem tradition—was, Mohammed thought, an enemy of the rights of mankind. Bourguiba returned to school determined to become politically active as a nationalist. A Tunisian could acquire true dignity, he felt, only in a free and independent country.

After Bourguiba finished school in Tunis, he went to Paris for legal training. He returned home in 1927, with two French law degrees, a French wife and a baby son.

"I don't hate the French," he reminded his friends, who were surprised at his marriage. "I hate only colonialism."

It was true that he didn't hate the French, and he knew that France had done some good things. He was careful to remember that even some of the colons shared his progressive ideas. Soon he developed a concrete programme for the Neo-Destour party. He didn't preach hatred of the French government, but instead advanced his own ideas and sought to carry his message to the remote ill-educated Arab villages.

The gist of this programme was to call for a gradual—not an immediate—withdrawal of French authority from Tunisia. There were two aspects to that authority, just as in Morocco. One covered domestic affairs, the other foreign.

Tunisia's domestic affairs—her police, her courts and her civil service—were all handled by Frenchmen under the direction of a French Resident General. The Bey of Tunis, the country's nominal ruler, was as completely a puppet of the French as was Morocco's Sultan. And for each member of the Bey's Cabinet there was a French "adviser" who actually made the decisions.

Tunisia's foreign affairs were controlled directly from Paris. France kept an army inside Tunisia's borders, and regarded the country's defence as part of the over-all defence of France. Tunisia was permitted to have no direct relations with other countries.

Bourguiba's programme for independence called first for home rule for Tunisia—the right to manage her domestic affairs. Then, when that had been accomplished, the country would be ready to move forward to full independence. It seemed to Bourguiba and his friends that this programme could be achieved by peaceful negotiation, and without bitterness. They looked forward to the day when a free Tunisia could live in harmony with France, for the best interests of both countries.

But the French authorities refused to consider negotiations of any kind with Tunisian nationalists. They soon came to regard Bourguiba as a dangerous enemy. In 1934 they exiled him to the desert. He was released two years later, but clapped into prison again in 1938. In that same year the Neo-Destour party was declared illegal.

Soon after Bourguiba was locked in his cell in the old military prison of Tunis, the Second World War exploded in Europe. France collapsed when the Nazis attacked, and the Germans promptly took over command in Tunisia. One of their first moves was to set Bourguiba free and invite him to join them against the Allies.

Bourguiba refused to do this, which proves that he had always meant what he said when he declared he didn't hate the French. He did, however, accept his freedom, and took the opportunity to speak over the German-controlled radio on Tunisia's right to independence. But he quietly and courageously urged his friends to stand behind the Allies, and to work toward the day when France and Tunisia would both be free of Nazi invaders. This is one reason why, when the Allies landed in Bizerta, they found friendly Arabs to welcome and assist them.

But when Tunisia was retaken from the Nazis, and restored to French control, one of the first things the French did was to arrest Bourguiba again. He escaped, and made his way to Cairo. Then he travelled widely, and in 1946 paid a visit to the United States. When he turned toward home again it was with new hope. There was much talk in the United Nations, and in the world at large, of freedom for colonial people. Bourguiba believed that the time had perhaps arrived when the French would be willing to talk reasonably about granting Tunisia at least a promise of future independence.

BOURGUIBA, THE BEY AND A MURDER

Bourguiba met two important figures when he reached Tunis.

One was Farhat Hached, a fellow leader in the struggle for freedom. Hached was a labour organizer who had made his union the best run and most powerful trades union in North Africa, and who also had the support of most other patriotic groups—not only the workers, but the old Destour, the still-outlawed Neo-Destour, the Jews and even the royal circles around the Bey of Tunis.

Hached was a calm, competent man who, like Bourguiba, wanted above all to unite the country. But his efforts to win decent wages for Arab workers had stirred up fierce hatred among the French colons who liked to hire native labour as cheaply as possible. A secret vigilante organization of colons called the Red Hand hated Hached in particular.

The other man Bourguiba saw was the Bey of Tunis.

The Bey was an elderly man. He had been over sixty when he reached the throne several years earlier, because the custom in Tunisia is to choose a new Bey from among the *oldest* members of the royal family. This, naturally, was a custom the French approved highly. It meant that each Bey was likely to be old-fashioned and behind the times, and therefore a feeble puppet in the hands of the French Resident General.

Sidi Mohammed Lamine Pasha, to give the Bey his full name, belongs to a family which began to rule Tunisia in 1705, after confused centuries of Turkish domination. His forebears occupied the throne during the heyday of the Barbary pirates, and in many ways the family seems to live still in those dark ages.

When Sidi Mohammed came to the throne he must have been the last monarch left in the world who kept a private troop of dwarfs, as oriental monarchs often did in feudal times. He loved to mix secret brews and potions in his laboratory, like a medieval alchemist. He knew no Western language and even his Arabic was primitive.

He wasn't an extravagant man—the French said he was too stupid even to know how to spend money —but the salary he received was enormous. And the hundreds of members of his family were all supported by public funds, because their position made it unseemly for them to do any work.

When I visited the Throne Room in the Dar El Bey, the royal palace in Tunis, what interested me most was a small projecting alcove with low windows. Directly underneath this lay a route into the market. Here the Bey, unobserved, could watch passers-by, like a child playing at being a spy.

This was the man to whom Bourguiba appealed for help. It might have seemed a foolish thing to do. Most nationalists despised the royal circle on the ground that most of its members were worthless parasites. The Bey didn't even have the authority of a religious leader, because—unlike the Sultan of Morocco—he doesn't claim descent from Mohammed and was not a head of the church.

But, in fact, the Bey had already made it clear to his close associates that he was interested in independence for his country. At least one of his sons had taken an active part in the nationalist movement. Even one of his daughters, married to a nationalist who was arrested by the French, gave the movement secret support. And, in any case, since the Bey was the country's nominal ruler, Bourguiba had no other choice. The help he wanted could be given only by the Bey and by no one else.

Bourguiba asked the old gentleman to seek the support of the United Nations on behalf of Tunisia's fight for freedom. The Bey, to the horrified astonishment of the French, agreed.

The French immediately put pressure on the Bey, to keep him quiet. Also they got rid of Bourguiba—for the time being. They exiled him first to a tiny island off the Tunisian coast, an island occupied only by a few lobstermen. Then, fearful that he might still be able to get in touch with his friends on the mainland, they transferred him to another island hundreds of miles away, off the northern coast of France.

A few months later Farhat Hached, the labour leader, was ambushed in broad daylight and brutally machine-gunned to death. His murderers were never caught, but they were almost certainly members of the sinister secret organization of French colons called the Red Hand.

Hached's death, following so quickly on Bourguiba's exile, was a tragedy for Tunisia and for France as well. It set off riots even in far-off Morocco, which caused hundreds of deaths and brought world-wide censure to France. In Tunisia it roused to fury many Arabs who, until then, had listened patiently and hopefully when Bourguiba and Hached both urged them to work peaceably toward independence. Hached had been a moderate and a splendid man.

The farms of French colons now began to be attacked by marauding bands of terrorists called *fellagha*. Some of the *fellagha* may have been ordinary bandits, who seized this opportunity for theft and looting. Others were nationalists. The French colons became convinced, in any case, that the angry Arabs had risen in a body to slay them all. They asked for more protection from the army, and new French troops arrived in Tunisia.

But the *fellagha* activity didn't stop. On the contrary, it increased. Tunisians killed; then Frenchmen killed in revenge; then Tunisians killed again. Political assassinations went on at the unbelievable rate of one per day.

THE TUNISIAN CASE

In the meantime, supported by nearly a dozen Asian-Arab nations, Tunisia was officially asking the United Nations to pass a resolution demanding that she be granted her independence within three years. The French response in the United Nations was angry.

The French delegation declared that Tunisia would never be ready for independence within that period, that France herself was planning reforms that ought to satisfy the protectorate and that France deserved to rule the country herself if only because she had already done so much for it.

French officials published figures to prove this last statement:

> Tunisia had practically no roads and only 117 miles of railway when France became her protector in 1881; now the country had 8,990 miles of road and 1,350 miles of railway.
>
> Two large dams had been built and more were planned. Already 45,000 acres of land were under irrigation.
>
> In 1881 there were only slightly more than a million acres of land in Tunisia planted to grain; now the figure was well over three million acres (of which Europeans owned 617,000).
>
> France contributed 58 per cent of Tunisia's total budget.

But the Tunisians could make out a good case for themselves too. I was in the country at about this time, and it was clear to me—as it was to any visitor —that there was no freedom of the press, or of speech, or assembly. Civil liberties were unknown. Everybody assumed as a matter of course that his mail was opened. There were about six thousand political prisoners in Saharan concentration camps, sent there without any process of law whatever.

I talked to one youthful lawyer who had recently been released from the inferno-like camp at Foum Tatahouime. There had been no explanation given to him when he was sent there, and none when he was released. He said living in Tunisia at that time was like living with a sword hanging over one's head by a thread, ready to drop at any moment.

By midsummer of 1954 Tunisia was perilously close to civil war. The support the nationalists had hoped to get from the United States and the United Nations was being offered instead by the Arab nations already grouped together into the Arab League —an organization that stood firmly against all colonialism and therefore, in effect, against the Western world. Religious leaders in Cairo were calling on all Moslems everywhere to boycott France "commercially, industrially, politically and culturally."

Then, in August, the realistic Mendès-France became France's new premier. At once events in Tunisia, as in Morocco at the same time, took a different and better course. The Premier himself flew to Tunis, lifted the ban on the Neo-Destour, announced that Bourguiba was free to leave his island exile and confer with government officials in France and promised Tunisia immediate home rule.

WHAT HAPPENED NEXT

If that promise had been honoured, France still might have a hand in Tunisia's government. If France had granted home rule at that moment, the nationalists might not have been strong enough to continue their fight until they won full independence. But the promise wasn't kept.

Most of the French colons were terrified at the prospect of being ruled by the Arabs they despised. The bankers of France feared that under Tunisian rule the country's economy—already in serious straits, partly because of a severe drought—would go completely to pieces. If that happened they thought their investments in Tunisia would become worthless, a circumstance which they were determined to prevent.

Those two groups, the colons and big financiers, together with men who dreaded the reforms Mendès-France had promised for Morocco, were powerful enough to force the new Premier out of office at the end of six brief months. And, with Mendès-France out of the way, the French government turned its back on the policies he had recommended for Tunisia and the rest of North Africa.

Now many angry Tunisians joined a Secret Committee for the Liberation of Tunisia. This committee didn't even try to seek help from the Western world. Instead it was definitely linked with the Arab League led by Egypt and later encouraged by the Soviet Union. Its members were ready to fight, with arms which they hoped to obtain from Cairo.

France realized that she was on the brink of catastrophe. In Tunisia, in Morocco, even in Algeria, the Arab populations were rising up against her. The door was open to rebellion on all fronts.

If that rebellion succeeded, France would lose everything. North Africa would of course no longer be under her control. But, worse than that, North Africa might become a springboard for attack against her. The powerful naval base at Bizerta, for example, might then be in the hands of forces unfriendly to France.

Suddenly the French leaders saw that, in all North Africa, Bourguiba could be their best ally. He had never given his support to the idea of an alliance of

Arab nations against the Western world. He was firmly anti-Communist. He had always said, in fact, that the Arab nations needed the West—needed the kind of technical, scientific and financial help that only the West could give.

By dealing with Bourguiba, the French leaders belatedly realized, they might ward off the worst of the dangers that threatened them.

One French official remarked about Bourguiba at that time, "For years we tried to ignore, suppress or discredit him, but finally we learned that this wouldn't work. Now we realize, and we admit, that Bourguiba is a great man."

Even in this emergency France didn't intend to give up any more than she had to. When her government leaders conferred with Bourguiba, they offered only the same home rule that Mendès-France had once promised. It would leave in French hands the control of Tunisia's foreign policy (so she couldn't ally herself with other Arab states) and the country's military defence. It meant that France would keep an army in Tunisia and retain authority over the Bizerta base.

But Bourguiba and his supporters shrewdly accepted the offer. Soon afterward a colourful ceremony took place in the blue and green Throne Room of the Bey's palace. Courtiers in long white, pink and yellow robes murmured their admiration for the gold-and-leather-bound documents prepared for the Bey's approval. The document made him absolute monarch over his country's domestic affairs. Outside the palace a crowd cheered, and Bourguiba was hailed by a joyous mob.

On the surface everything seemed pleasant. France believed she had made the best of a bad bargain.

But the bargaining wasn't over. Bourguiba had accepted the offer of home rule only because he believed in negotiating for independence one step at a time. He fully intended to move forward to the next and final step. But some fanatic Tunisians called him a "traitor" (for negotiating with the French), accused him of selling out his own country and attacked his followers, as well as the French, with renewed terrorism. Still Bourguiba waited, refusing to break off his patient talks. He was still convinced that independence could be won without outright war.

Events proved Bourguiba right. Morocco was demanding independence too. The Arab League's clamour on behalf of the two Moslem nations grew louder each day. Even the United States, so reluctant to oppose France, now appeared to be giving the nationalists encouragement—so much so that furious colons wrecked the U.S. Consulate in Tunis.

Tunisia's time was ripening. Every day more and more French faced up to the fact that Tunisia would never be satisfied with mere home rule, and that Tunisia now had powerful friends. Finally a formula for independence was agreed upon. On March 20, 1956, about two weeks after Morocco became free, the French protectorate at last came to an end. Tunisia's independence had been won.

Shortly afterward the country had a new national assembly, whose members were chosen in free elections. Then, in July 1957, the assembly dethroned the elderly Bey, declared an end to the monarchy and proclaimed Tunisia a republic. Its first President, elected without opposition, was Habib Bourguiba.

A NEW COUNTRY FACES THE FUTURE

Tunisia, newly independent after seventy-five years of French control, faced all the problems that must be met by every new country, and some extra ones as well.

The chief problems were:

1. Poverty
2. Ill-feeling among the various groups of the population
3. Unsettled relations with France.

Tunisia's poverty, at the time she gained her independence, was severe. She had never been a rich country. Even in normal years one-third of her people were undernourished. Furthermore the country's population was increasing rapidly, owing in part to the excellent French public-health programme which sharply cut down disease and the death rate. This meant that every year the country had more and more mouths to feed. It meant that more people would go hungry every year, unless food production improved, or unless the nation's income increased so that she could afford to import more grain, meat and other products.

But to improve food production—even if no new droughts occurred—would require better farming methods and better farm equipment. To increase the nation's income, by increasing the number of jobs available, would require new businesses and new industries. Tunisia herself didn't have the money for either of these programmes, and unemployment was increasing.

As to domestic ill-feeling, there were Arabs who still felt resentful of the French. There were Moslems, under the influence of the Arab League, who resented Jews. And this resentment was returned in good measure.

Many Frenchmen were trying to sell their farms so that they could leave the country, and few new French-owned businesses were opening up. Jewish-owned businesses were closing, as many Jews tried to leave Tunisia. This too had a serious effect on the country's economy.

The government did its best to smooth out these tangles. It wanted, in its own best interests, to guard the rights and investments of all its people, and its main object is to create a country where Arabs, French and Jews can all live in harmony together.

"There were Frenchmen who imagined that they would all be chucked into the sea the moment we became independent," Bourguiba said in his brisk way to an American reporter several months after the protectorate ended. "Nobody's been chucked into the sea," he went on, "and there isn't a more peaceful city in the world today than Tunis."

But the countryside, away from the big cities and especially along the Algerian border, was not quite so peaceful. And this brings us to Tunisia's third major problem: her unsettled relations with France. These hinge to an extent on events in Algeria and may thus remain unsettled for some time.

SOME TUNISIAN PROBLEMS

"Tunisia is a small state," Bourguiba said recently, "but we intend to make it a model for all other Arab countries: a country based on social justice and respect for the human person."

On the domestic front, one of the first things that his government did was to strike at some old Moslem traditions which, he felt, had long hampered human dignity, and especially the dignity of women.

For instance, Tunisia has given women the vote, abolished polygamy and easy divorce, and prohibited marriages of girls under fifteen years of age. It also abolished the old Koranic courts which had always settled all cases of personal and family relationships. Now these courts have been merged with the country's regular civil courts, and cases are being disposed of according to modern laws rather than by ancient Moslem tradition.

"The reforms we have undertaken are very bold, and have naturally met with some opposition from the 'Old Turbans,'" Bourguiba said, referring to the most conservative group of the population. "But the vast majority of our people are in favour of them."

Tunisian officials have also drawn up plans for new schools, new dams and new irrigation projects. They explored methods for exploiting more fully the country's resources and giving better opportunities to the large new groups of educated Tunisians. But all this costs money and the bedrock problem of the country is still its poverty.

Other UN members have already supported the

new nation with words of encouragement. But
Tunisia needs more than that, or she may slip still
farther into poverty. Her standard of living, already
low for much of her population, may fall still lower.
In that case, as one observer said, "Nobody can tell
what the end will be." Tunisians, grown desperate,
may turn away from such a moderate leader as
Bourguiba and follow extremists who might promise,
for example, to seize all French-owned land and
distribute it among native farmers. That, of course,
could cause serious trouble and a desperate disloca-
tion of the country's economy.

So the fate of Tunisia depends at least in part on
the wisdom and good will of outsiders.

TWO ANCIENT CAPITALS: TUNIS
AND CARTHAGE

Tunis is one of the oldest capital cities in the world.
There was an army base here in the fourth century,
built by a Sicilian who hoped to destroy neighbouring Carthage. But, for all its age, it doesn't strike the
visitor as having much character. Its population of
about four hundred thousand includes large numbers of French and Italians. Only in the Arabs' own
crowded quarter are there sights that are purely
and colourfully Arabian.

The city stands at the narrow end of a long
funnel-shaped bay, and its protected harbour has
always been a much-sought prize in time of war.
The last armies who fought over it were the Allied

and Axis forces in the Second World War. Then bombardments ruined the wharves and laid waste most of the surrounding buildings. But repair work started soon after the Allied triumph in North Africa —a triumph celebrated by a huge victory parade through Tunis' streets. Dwight D. Eisenhower, then the Allied commander-in-chief, was on hand to review the troops that marched through the rubble that day, under a shower of flowers tossed by the excited Tunisians along the route. Today the harbour of Tunis has been so completely rebuilt that no sign of bomb damage remains.

Opposite the city's railway station stands a gleaming monument "To Science and Agriculture," honouring the two fields in which Tunis sees her hopes for the future. But a more impressive monument to science is Tunis' Pasteur Institute. There, for many years until his death in 1935, the French Nobel prize winner, Charles Nicolle, using himself as a guinea pig, studied several dangerous African diseases. His work on trachoma, which causes blindness and afflicts vast numbers of Africans, was particularly valuable. Thousands of people throughout the country can see today because Nicolle gave his life to the work carried on in this building.

The blue and white terraces of the Arab quarter cover the hillside that rises above the city's waterfront avenues. Its markets are divided into sections, each devoted to a single product: copperware, perfume, jewellery, honey cakes and so on. An Arab market is really nothing more or less than an outdoor department store, where goods are often made—as well as sold—right on the premises.

In one of the squares, where faithful Moslems gather to feast after dusk during the month of Ramadan, the visitor can almost always see a noisy Arabic version of a Punch and Judy show. Arabs, who are extremely fond of this performance, call it *Karagousee*.

During the spring this whole native town smells of jasmine, which is considered a lucky flower. Every merchant, every small boy, wears a sprig of the flower tucked behind his ear or carries a flower in his fingers, twirling it and sniffing at it as he walks.

The ruins of Carthage, only a few miles outside of Tunis, are not much to see. But visitors like to wander among the fragments of ancient stone still littering the hills above the Gulf of Carthage, and recall the legend of the city's founding. According to this, Dido, a Phoenician princess, first landed here with a group of her people, and asked the natives if she might rest for a while before going on her way. She promised them that she would need only a tiny piece of land—a mere patch that could be bound within the skin of an ox. The generous Berbers made her welcome, whereupon Dido cut an ox skin into threadlike ribbons and laid them out, end to end, to enclose a large area. Within that circle, the legend says, Carthage was built—and the Berbers could never dislodge the people who had tricked them into giving up so much of their land.

Near Carthage is a pretty and charming village called Sidi Bou Said, which has become the home of writers and artists from all over the world. Its buildings are almost all white, with blue paintwork standing out against the whitewashed plaster like sprays of blue cornflowers.

History has left some odd footprints in this area. For instance, the leaning tower of Pisa is supposed to have been built out of stone carried to Italy from Carthage.

King Louis IX of France, who led several Crusades against the Moslems and earned the title of St. Louis, died in Carthage after an assault on the city in 1270. Now the local Arabs regard this long-ago Christian enemy as a holy man, or marabout.

KAIROUAN, THE HOLY CITY

From Tunis I drove inland to Kairouan, the oldest Arabic city in North Africa. It was founded in 673 by Sidi Okba, leader of an Arab invading force that pushed its way clear across the top of the continent to the Atlantic. The great mosques, with their minarets and cupolas, lie deep within the shabby precincts of the old town.

This is one of the holiest cities in the Moslem world. Three pilgrimages to Kairouan are the equivalent of one to Mecca. It has no connection with the famous mosque called Kairouyine in the Moroccan city of Fez, but the names of both the mosque and the city come from the Arabic word *karwâne*, which means "relay point," and gives us our word "caravan." Both Kairouan and Fez were, of course, relay points on old routes taken by camel caravans.

The most outstanding mosque of the city of Kairouan is the one dedicated to Sidi Okba himself. It
is a mad extravaganza, with hundreds of columns,
almost none of them alike. Nothing matches. But
visitors are usually more curious about the so-called
Barber's Mosque, which also serves as the tomb of a
man said to have been a close friend of the Prophet
Mohammed. According to the old Moslem story,
the man was buried clutching in his hand three hairs
from the Prophet's beard, and these hairs are still
there.

All the mosques of this city are open to infidels—
that is, to non-Moslems. The Tunisians say the
French "desecrated" them by forcing their way into
the buildings. Having once been entered by Christians, they have been open to Christians ever since.

The sook (bazaar or market) in Kairouan is not
so picturesque or enclosed as those in Morocco, and
it seems cleaner. Grain, vegetables and other foods
don't lie directly on the ground, but on straw mats
or in baskets. Kairouan rugs are worth a special
look. They are woven of fine wool and dyed in
beautiful colours by master craftsmen. The Tunisian
government encourages these artists to keep alive
this ancient Arabic art.

Kairouan was the scene of many fierce battles
during its early days. Arab historians also tell us that
one ruler, after a victorious engagement outside the
city, returned with ten thousand enemy heads "for
the children to use as toys and footballs." Kairouan's
many conquerors were proud of this Arabic capital
and decorated it with lavish gardens, palaces and
man-made lakes. In those lakes, present-day guides

'Algiers looks so much like one of the French coastal towns across the Mediterranean'

Great efforts are being made to irrigate the desert wastes of Libya in order to grow more food. The lower photograph shows ploughing taking place on an experimental farm

will tell you, swans and gilded barges once floated among perfumed fountains.

Outside the city I drove past Roman monuments without number. Anybody digging a well in this area, or even planting crops, will almost certainly unearth bits of Roman marble. You can fill your pockets with loot—genuine antiquities—in an afternoon. Each one is a reminder of the wonderful things the Romans did when Tunisia was the Roman province of *Africa Proconsularis*. Maps are still in use today that follow line by line old Roman maps which charted the best areas for irrigation and olive culture.

Nearby is the town of Hammamet, which the Romans called by the quaint name of Putput. Many artists live in its enchanting gardens. Beyond is the seaside town of Sousse, which was called Hadrumetum in Roman days. Here Caesar landed in 46 B.C. to undertake his African campaign. He stumbled as he stepped out on to the shore, and his followers grew pale with fright because they regarded this as an ill omen. But Caesar quickly threw himself flat— as if that had been his deliberate intention—and kissed a handful of sand he grabbed up. "I hold you in my grasp, O Africa!" he shouted. The ill omen was transformed into a promise of the victory that lay ahead of him.

Still farther south along the coast is Sfax, an olive-oil port. The flat surrounding country has been described as being like some vast rug woven of only three colours—the ash-grey colour of the earth, the silver-grey of olive tree trunks and the green of their foliage. No grass grows in the broad bare paths between the widely spaced rows of trees, and nothing else is planted in this area where every precious drop of water must be used to nourish Tunisia's most valuable agricultural crop. But Sfax itself is a vividly colourful place—a riot of gardens crowded with pomegranate and pistachio trees, roses, geraniums and lianas.

In fact, all the towns along this stretch of the Tunisian coastline would be delightful places to live in except for one thing: They are all regular victims of a hot, unpleasant, enervating wind called the sirocco.

A HANDFUL OF TUNISIAN ISLANDS

Islands dot the whole Tunisian coast, and each one has its own special flavour. Some are inhabited only by herds of wild goats, thousands of wild rabbits and other creatures, living in jungle-like growths of flowering trees.

Many were once famous pirate strongholds. Two of them, named Zembra and Zembretta—but usually called, together, the Zimbres—guard the Gulf of Tunis and even today are used as hiding places by smugglers, modern descendants of the Barbary corsairs.

The Island of Roumédia, farther south, is famous for the camels that are bred and trained there.

But Tunisia's most fascinating island is Djerba. Most historians think the ancient Greek writer, Homer, was describing this place when he wrote

about the Land of the Lotus-Eaters. Here his great
hero, Ulysses, stayed for seven years. Those who eat
the lotus, Homer wrote, never want to leave the
island, because the "divine nectarous" juice makes
them forget everything they have ever known in
their past. Perhaps Homer didn't know that the
lotus is really nothing but a small brownish berry
with very little taste.

Today the island's blue, white and yellow houses
nestle among olive and pimento trees, and its inhabitants work at spice-making and rug-weaving.
Each family of Djerba weavers has its own designs
and its own secret dyes, carefully handed down from
one generation to the next.

On this island, where a large colony of Jews has
lived for many centuries, is one of the most sacred
of all synagogues. It is said to be built over a stone
brought here from the temple of Solomon, at the
time this was destroyed by Nebuchadnezzar. For
hundreds of years Jews have made pilgrimages to
this temple, and it is still a place of pilgrimage today.

Like Tunisia itself, this little island is a true crossroads of north-south and east-west Mediterranean
traffic. Like Tunisia it stands, as it has always stood,
at the centre of the pulsating Mediterranean world.

Whatever the future may hold for Tunisia, then,
it is safe to say that this North-Africa-in-miniature
will always be full of interest. It is still, as it has been
since the days of Carthage, a meeting place for the
ideas, the conflicts and the people of three continents
—Africa, Europe and Asia.

7

War Comes to Algeria

In November, 1954, armed rebellion broke out against French authority in Algeria. The affair seemed minor at first, and then grew serious. Eight Frenchmen were murdered in localities spread over a wide area. Garrisons were cut off and remote army outposts attacked.

The French government in Paris was astounded. There was trouble in Morocco and Tunisia at the same time, and many Frenchmen were beginning to realize that those protectorates would never be satisfied with anything less than complete freedom from France. But Algeria had always seemed to be safe and quiet.

Moreover, Algeria was not a protectorate. Politically it was a part of France, just as much as Normandy or Brittany. Algerians were, by law, the same as Frenchmen. If they shot down Frenchmen they were shooting their fellow citizens.

This is why the flare-up in Algeria was such a shocking and startling event. It was an act of civil war. In Paris it was compared to the attack on Fort

Sumter in the United States—the burst of cannon shot that marked the beginning of the American Civil War in 1861. And when people in Algeria talked of wanting their freedom from France, Paris said it was impossible—just as the American government in Washington had once declared that the Southern states could not have their "freedom," could not be allowed to secede from the country.

France swiftly roused herself to put down this rebellion. She flew paratroopers across the Mediterranean and landed them in Algeria, and otherwise strongly increased her forces. Within a week she claimed that the revolt was over.

But it wasn't over. It spurted up again almost immediately, and it is still going on as these words are being written. Thousands of men, women and children have lost their lives since the fighting began. Thousands of farms have been destroyed—buildings burned, crops set ablaze.

The native population of Algeria is determined to make its country free and independent. France is just as determined not to lose an area that is roughly four times larger than France itself, and that is vital to French interests.

The story behind this revolt is one of the most significant in North Africa. It has its roots deep in the history of this land and its inhabitants.

WHAT IS ALGERIA?

Only the hilly coastal region of Algeria is capable of supporting a sizeable population. And this area has become terrifically overcrowded, since Algeria's population increases at the staggering rate of 250,000 a year. Here, in the 3 per cent of Algeria that is arable, live the majority of the country's nine million people. Of these about six million are Arabs, about two million are Berbers. The rest are Europeans, mostly French.

Of the Berbers, the largest group is that of a sturdily independent people called Kabyles. The Kabyles are herdsmen and olive growers, possessed of an ancient culture, who live in two adjoining areas along the coast. They are so crowded together that some farmers don't even own a whole olive tree. They have to be content with branches of a tree shared by several owners.

Other smaller Berber groups, interesting because they differ strikingly from most North Africans, are the blue-veiled Tuareg of the Sahara and the M'zabites.

The M'zabites are a survival of one of the small fanatical sects characteristic of Moslems. They live very much to themselves, in a little group of five towns a couple of hundred miles south of Algiers. Ghardaïa, the largest of these, is their unofficial capital. They have remarkably pale skins, even for Berbers, and remarkably strict religious beliefs. All amusements—even listening to music—are taboo. But perhaps the outstanding thing about the M'zabites is their genius for business.

In the great days of caravan travel they made the oases around Ghardaïa a rich centre of trade—so much so that a single acre of ground, even if arid, came to be worth a great deal of money. Today the men of this group often go to the coastal cities to work as bankers or traders for a while, and then—when they have grown wealthy—return to their desert villages and their pious, solemn life. If one of them dies while he is away from home, his body is shipped back to his village for burial. M'zabite corpses have even made this long journey by taxi-cab, if no other means of travel was available.

ALGERIA BECOMES FRENCH

Algeria's history was for a long time closely allied to that of Morocco and Tunisia, which flank her on each side.

Phoenicians, Romans, Vandals, Arabs, Spaniards and Turks all came here in turn, and left their mark. Probably all of them drank the Algerian wine and ate the Algerian figs which today, along with iron ore and phosphates, are still the country's chief products. But none of them really unified the country into a single entity. Even the Turkish dey who sat on the throne of Algiers, when this city became a Barbary pirate capital, never claimed authority over the whole territory we now call Algeria. Nor was he recognized as the religious leader.

By 1830, when French warships first appeared off the port of Algiers, the vast territory of Algeria still consisted of scattered Arab and Berber communities, not even united by any religious authority. Each community lived pretty much in its own way. France, setting out to make a colonial empire, had to conquer them one by one.

French soldiers were firmly established in Algiers exactly twenty days after they first landed near the city. They entered it triumphantly through a gate gruesomely bedecked with the heads of Frenchmen who had been seized from trading vessels and murdered by the Algiers pirates. Within a month France was at work civilizing the locality, which badly needed civilizing.

The rest of the country took longer to subdue, even with the help of two new forces which the French organized. One of these was the famous Foreign Legion, composed of volunteers from all over the world. Most of the Legionnaires were tough fighting men, who preferred war to any other occupation, or who had gone to Algiers because they were in trouble back home.

The other new French force was a Camel Corps. Members are sometimes known as meharists because they ride specially bred, specially trained dromedaries called meharas. French soldiers had never seen dromedaries before they went to Algeria, and at first they laughed uproariously at these awkward swaying beasts. But they learned to respect them as the best of all desert mounts, and the only means by which they could successfully pursue camel-mounted natives to their remote desert strongholds.

One group of natives, led by a gallant sheikh who kept his people constantly on the move—they formed a huge caravan, a kind of nomad city—held out against the French for thirteen years. And certain tribes in the interior were not really conquered for another decade or longer.

Meanwhile France made the northern part of

Algeria officially a part of France. The French didn't leave a native ruler on the throne, as in Morocco and Tunisia, or claim Algeria as a "protectorate." They declared that it actually belonged to France—lock, stock and barrel.

France divided the hilly coastal area into three departments (we would call them states) and gave them the same status as the departments (or states) of France itself. Their inhabitants eventually became full-fledged French citizens, with the right to elect representatives to the French Assembly in Paris. Later the southern part of the country, much bigger than the northern, was organized into the so-called Southern Territories, which had a slightly different status. They were not a part of France, or ruled directly from Paris. Instead they were a kind of subcolony of northern Algeria, officially ruled from Algiers but actually ruled by the French army.

In the meantime, French colonists were settling along the coast and in the green hills behind the shore. They were in many ways real pioneers, like the settlers who came to the wilderness of the New World. They found themselves, in the words of one newcomer, in "a marsh of thick, tangled and impenetrable bush, gigantic grass tufts, prickly shrubs, dwarf palms, growing in a soggy ground into which one sank at every step."

There were no roads, because there had never been any need for roads until they came. The natives had no carriages, and were shocked at the very idea of using spirited horses to pull vehicles. The heat was often unendurable to settlers accustomed to the

cool climate of France. And there was fever. As
many as one-third of the colonists died of fever every
year in the beginning. Discouragement and fear of
hostile natives sent hundreds of others home during
the first half-century of French control.

But within those first fifty years the stubborn colonists who remained in Algeria transformed a great
part of the coastal area into a garden spot. They
shipped vast quantities of grain, olives, figs and other
products to the homeland. Eventually, of course,
they came to own a great deal of the best land in
Algeria—some of which they had made best by their
own efforts at irrigation and scientific agriculture.

After that first difficult half-century the process
of Europeanizing the land went on rapidly. An excellent health programme was set up. Good railways
and fine new roads were built. Cities took on the
look and atmosphere of French towns at home.

Many French families have been living in Algeria
for several generations. Like Americans whose families have lived in the United States for a hundred
years or more, they felt that they had helped to
create the nation and that it was their own. They no
longer felt like foreigners there. They felt completely
at home, in a land which they took for granted
would remain for ever a part of France. And they
paid little attention to the Arabs.

Meantime many Arabs—and some Berbers too,
especially the city dwellers—"became French" in
manners and speech and dress. Native clothes were
seldom seen in Algerian cities, except perhaps in the
native quarter. An Arab boy who managed to go to
college in Paris usually returned home looking and

talking exactly like his Paris-born college mates. He read French newspapers and saw French plays. Many Arabs were, in other words, "assimilated."

Many young Arab girls, particularly students, went unveiled. Some of them took jobs as salesgirls in the shops, or as servants in European homes. Some even sat publicly in the cafés.

Arab workmen, furthermore, often went to France to live for a time, or to settle there permanently. They formed large Algerian settlements in Paris and in French mining towns like Lille. This coming and going helped to give the impression that the two countries were closely united in every way—really two parts of the same nation.

Native Algerians also seemed to have equal rights so far as government was concerned. They made up half the number of representatives which Algeria sent to the French Assembly. They entirely filled one house of the local Assembly, which met in Algiers, and partially filled the other.

But all these signs of French-Algerian "equality" were on paper only. In actual fact there was very little equality. And the native Algerians knew it.

They knew, for example, that what the colons really wanted was cheap, unskilled, uneducated Arab labour—not Arab guests in their drawing-rooms. Every time the Arabs heard the French use that insulting word, "*salesarabes*"—and it was used more often in Algiers than anywhere else in North Africa—they were reminded of how much the French despised them.

Naturally the native Algerians resented this. They also resented other things, such as that:

1. Their so-called "free" elections were carefully controlled so that only pro-French Arabs could be chosen as deputies to the Assemblies in Paris and Algiers. The French themselves scornfully called these puppet deputies "*Beni-ouis-ouis*," or "Yes-men." Very few Arabs were permitted to hold jobs in the Algerian civil service.

2. The colons, although not all of them were wealthy, owned two-thirds of the arable land in Algeria, and controlled the entire wine production, which is the basis of the country's economy.

3. French interests also controlled banks, shipping, mines, local transportation, public utilities and most of the grain production.

4. A few Algerians may have been well-to-do, but the vast majority was wretchedly poor. Sixty per cent of the native population, outside the cities, was officially classed as "destitute."

5. Education among the natives was so scant (the French government never gave the country a penny for Arab schools until 1952) that only about 2 per cent of them could read or write.

All this helps to explain why the Algerians broke out in revolt against France, and why this revolt, which began with guerrilla terrorism, developed into a fight for full independence.

Several nationalist organizations, including a fairly strong Communist party, took part in the struggle. When these groups combined in an effort to bring Algeria's case before the United Nations in 1955, other Arab nations supported them. But France refused to discuss the subject in the UN.

No other country, France declared, had the right

to interfere in the Algerian situation, because it was strictly a French problem. "Suppose," France said in effect, "Alaska wanted to separate itself from the rest of the United States. Would that be a case for the UN to decide? Of course not. It would be a case for Americans—including Alaskans—to work out for themselves. The Algerian situation is similar. It is a problem for Frenchmen—including Algerians— to settle without outside interference." And indeed there was much that seemed reasonable in this argument—if the French really showed good will.

The United States supported the French (for the same reasons which led her to support France, somewhat reluctantly, in the struggles over Morocco and Tunisia), and this made Americans extremely unpopular among Algerian nationalists for a time. Determined to fight for their freedom if they could not win it otherwise, the Algerians looked for aid from the other Arab nations. They made it clear, in fact, that they would accept help from any source willing to give it, including Communists.

One rebel leader declared that he would not refuse the offer of guns and ammunition from the Soviet Union or even "from the devil," if help could be obtained nowhere else.

A WAR OF WORDS AND TERRORISM

When France insisted upon settling the Algerian problem herself, she was taking on a heavy job. The problem has no easy solution. First the government

tried to appease the nationalists with promises of
reform, but then the colons rose in wrath. They
wanted no reforms which would give Arabs more
power and wealth at their expense.

And when the government tried to suppress the
nationalists by force of arms, the nationalists learned
new techniques of terrorism. French soldiers and
French colons both learned to fear the swift Arab or
Berber raiders who usually appeared at nightfall,
and disappeared again before they could be caught
—after having destroyed a farm, assaulted a small
army convoy, staged a swift riot or blown up a
stretch of railway.

Headlines in the world's newspapers, day after
day, reported the steady stream of ugly "incidents"
taking place in Algeria.

Thousands of lives were lost as the murderous con-
flict went on. The French had to increase their army
in Algiers to a strength of more than three hundred
thousand men—a lot. There were more Algerian
casualties than French, but the cost to France—in
economic strain and political unrest as well as lives
—was enormous. All this was, incidentally, of direct
interest to the United States not only from a
humanitarian point of view but because the French
had to take many of their troops out of Europe in
order to reinforce their detachments in Algiers.
This in turn meant that NATO—the international
force which keeps Communism at bay in western
Europe—was gravely weakened.

Algeria's neighbours, Tunisia and Morocco, also
watched what was going on in Algeria. When these
countries gained their own freedom from France, in

the spring of 1956, their leaders set to work to aid in settling the Algerian problem. They wanted their Moslem brothers in Algeria to share in the freedom their own countries had won. And they knew, besides, that France would have a pretext for keeping armed forces stationed in both Morocco and Tunisia so long as war was going on in the territory that lay between them. They knew, in other words, that until there was peace in all three countries, there could never be real peace in any one.

The Algerian side of the fighting was directed mostly from Cairo, where most of the Algerian leaders were living in exile. They had had to flee from Algeria, of course. The fact that they lived in Cairo and had close relations with outspoken nationalists there led the French to think, apparently with good reason, that the Nasser government was a major force behind the Algerian rebels. They got money and arms from Egypt. Shiploads of smuggled ammunition managed to reach Algerian ports from Egypt, and got into rebel hands. The French were furious. This was one reason for the great crisis over the Suez Canal a year later. The Algerian revolt, seemingly so minor at first, had repercussions all the way from Washington to the Middle East.

But let us get back to Algeria itself, and its close neighbours. The Sultan of Morocco and Habib Bourguiba, Tunisia's patient leader, seeing that the situation was getting more out of control day by day, decided to make some kind of intervention, if possible. They were wholeheartedly on the Algerian side but they wanted a peaceful settlement with France if they could get it. They decided among other things that it might be a good idea to consult with some of the Algerian exiles in Cairo, to see if any basis of negotiation with the French was possible. At first, the French refused point-blank to have anything to do with such a conference. They denied that any Algerian "rebels" had a right to represent Algeria.

But anyway, the Sultan and Bourguiba went ahead with their plans. They invited five leading Algerian nationalists to meet with them, so that they might act as go-betweens or intermediaries. The five Algerians duly arrived in Rabat, the capital of Morocco, from Cairo, and had preliminary consultations with the Sultan. Conversations with Bourguiba, which would be much more important, were to follow. And they were scheduled to take place in Tunis during a state visit by the Sultan of Morocco to Tunisia, so that all the negotiators could meet together.

Then, on their way to Tunis to keep the rendezvous, the five Algerians were kidnapped by the French!—one of the most astounding episodes in modern history.

The Algerians—one of them was military commander of the Algerian National Liberation Front, another the political director and another the Algerian rebel envoy to the UN—had planned to go from Rabat to Tunis by boat. But their ship was seized by the French navy off Algiers. The excuse was that it was smuggling arms. So the Algerians had to change plans suddenly and their Moroccan hosts chartered a 'plane for them. The pilot was French, but the 'plane had been ordered on the authority of the Sultan of Morocco, and nobody suspected a plot.

The 'plane took off on schedule early in the morning of October 22, 1956, shortly after the Sultan's own 'plane set out for Tunisia. It made a refuelling stop on the island of Majorca, and by late afternoon was taking off again for Tunis, where it was expected to land three and a half hours later.

Thomas F. Brady, a *New York Times* reporter, was one of the newspapermen travelling by the chartered 'plane. Along with other reporters he talked to the Algerians during the trip, and found them "relaxed and cheerful." None of the passengers knew that the 'plane's pilot received a secret radio message while they were flying over the Mediterranean.

That message, from French headquarters in Algiers, ordered the pilot to bring his 'plane down in Algiers—not in Tunis. And the pilot was apparently glad to assist in the conspiracy. He told the stewardess to keep the passengers occupied, so that they wouldn't notice a change of direction. Then he circled over the sea until the hour arrived when the passengers expected to reach Tunis. When the proper time came he brought the 'plane down—in Algiers!

The *Times* reporter, describing the event, wrote that none of the passengers "had any suspicion of their whereabouts when the 'plane touched the ground. Then the interior lights went out and we could see armoured cars with spotlights and truckloads of gendarmes with submachine guns following us as we taxied to a halt."

They still didn't know they were at the Algiers airport when "suddenly there was a gendarme in the 'plane with a tommy gun."

One by one the passengers were forced to jump to the ground, hands over their heads. And the Algerians were thrown into jail.

Naturally, the Moroccans and Tunisians—to say nothing of the unfortunate Algerians—were outraged by this highhanded manoeuvre, but there was nothing they could do about it. One Moroccan official called it "an unspeakable act of piracy," and the Sultan himself declared that France had insulted him personally, by seizing men who had trusted themselves to his hospitality. It was a worse affront to his honour, the Sultan declared, than his removal from the throne. Bourguiba summoned the French Ambassador in Tunisia and warned him that now the whole of North Africa might have to engage in a new "test of force" with France. So plans for a negotiated settlement with Algeria had to be called off.

AFTERMATH OF THE KIDNAPPING

The revolt hasn't stopped, although the kidnapping seemed to take the heart out of the rebel movement for a time. After all, the rebels had lost five of their most important leaders—their general staff. They were like an army without a head.

Even so, in the period from November 6 to 26, immediately after the kidnapping, forty-one French soldiers and twenty European civilians were killed by terrorists. Algerian casualties—for dead alone—in the same period were 698. Pillage, looting, arson occurred every day. Late in November, Bourguiba appealed to the UN to step in and end the "butchery." And French relations with both Tunisia and Morocco were set back.

Seen in retrospect, the toll caused by the Algerian revolt has been terrible. In two years of fighting 896 farms and 229 schools have been destroyed, more than 20,000 head of cattle stolen, 11,225 acres of crops destroyed and more than 167,000 fruit trees and 3,200,000 grapevines ruined. But this is as nothing compared to the human loss. Violence breeds violence, and practically the whole of Algeria is still in a state of chaos.

The French, from their own point of view, had no choice but to act as they did. They were fighting to preserve what they thought was their own. And much in the French record in Algeria has been admirable. If it had not been for the shortsightedness of the local colons, as well as reactionary lawmakers in Paris, the uprising might have been averted. Now nobody knows what the end will be.

THREE ALGERIAN CITIES AND AN "AFRICAN POMPEII"

The Algerian countryside will probably, for a long time to come, bear brutal scars of fighting. Broken pipes have injured irrigation systems. Roads have been torn up and railways wrecked. French farmers have let their acres go untended, because they feared that if they did raise crops, the rebels would destroy them. But the big cities on the coast, despite much sabotage, do not show a great deal of damage.

Algiers, the capital (with a population of over three hundred thousand), is by far the most important of these cities. The most interesting thing about Algiers—apart from its long and lively history—is that it looks so much like one of the French coastal towns across the Mediterranean.

Here you can see many things which are characteristic of the best of France—boulevard cafés, neatly combed gardens behind black iron fences, steep mansard roofs and pavement kiosks full of gay posters. It has good bookshops and good restaurants —the French always believe in feeding the mind and body both.

But, behind its French awning, Algiers is still an Arab city. It is built in layers, or tiers, of white houses, rising one above the other. Standing at a window in the Kasbah, or Old Town, in the top tier, and looking down on the scene below, is like standing on a balcony and looking down on a crowded oriental stage.

The Kasbah itself doesn't have much colour any more. Some of its oldest houses have even been replaced by modern apartment houses. But there is plenty of colour in the stories a guide tells you as you stroll through its narrow, mysterious streets. One of the most famous former "residents" of the city, for example, was Miguel de Cervantes, the Spanish author of *Don Quixote*. He was held prisoner here for five years until the pirates who captured him were paid a ransom for his release.

The boulevard cafés of Algiers are crowded during the sunset hour, when the pavements become littered with the peanut shells tossed aside by people sipping drinks at the tiny tables. But by eight o'clock at night the tables are empty and the streets are quiet. Unlike most North African cities, Algiers seems to go to bed at an early hour—it has practically no night life at all.

The second most important seaport of Algeria is Oran, which looks like a dusty old Arab town but is actually a rapidly growing European city with few Moslem inhabitants. Spain held this place for two hundred years, after seizing it in 1509, and it still has a Spanish flavour. There are not many places in North Africa that have bullfights, but you can see them here. A great deal of Algeria's valuable wine production is shipped from this busy port.

Constantine, on the dry plains inland from the coast and not far from the Tunisian border, was an important trade centre even in the days of the Phoenicians. And it remained important during all the many stages of Algerian history. It was a favourite spot for American GI's in World War II.

The most striking sight here is a long chasm, or gorge—nearly five hundred feet deep and almost as wide—called the Rhumel. It splits the city in two along a snakelike line, as if a wavering hand had sliced through the earth with a huge knife. Since the days of the Romans the people of Constantine have had to bridge this chasm, and the oldest of the several bridges crossing it today stands where an ancient Roman bridge once stood.

But for real Roman ruins—and the most famous in all North Africa—the visitor has to go a little farther south to a place called Timgad, founded in about the year 100 B.C. Here archaeologists have laid bare remarkably complete buildings—a theatre, a forum, a library, public baths and temples— standing along roads that can still be clearly traced. It is quite easy to imagine, walking among these ruins, how proudly the ancient Romans lived in their African colony. In fact, Timgad has given us so much information about Rome that it has been compared to Italy's famous ruins at Pompeii, and it is sometimes called the "African Pompeii."

Not far south of Timgad the real desert begins, the great Sahara that spreads across half the continent. Every North African country has its own share of the Sahara, but Algeria's is biggest and includes such famous oases as Biskra, the legendary "Garden of Allah."

Also in Algeria are two of the Sahara's greatest expanses of pure sand, called the Grand Erg Occidental and Grand Erg Oriental, or Great Western Emptiness and Great Eastern Emptiness. Here too are this vast desert's largest mountainous regions. One of them is the Tassili-n-Ajjer, which is notable for having lakes with good water in its rugged hills —lakes teeming with fish. Another is the mass of craggy peaks called the Hoggar, home of some of the blue-veiled Tuareg, whom we will visit in the next chapter.

If the Sahara could ever be irrigated and made

fertile, the history of the continent—perhaps the history of the whole world—might be changed. For years people have dreamed of bringing water to the Saharan wastes, and scientific research toward this end goes on all the time. But the technical difficulties are almost insurmountable.

Water is important in the Sahara; so is another fluid—oil. Drilling for oil has already begun, and rich strikes are anticipated. Also the Sahara is believed to have other important mineral resources—copper, iron, uranium, tungsten, tin and coal. As soon as the possibility of large-scale oil and mineral development became known, the French government set up a new administration to control the whole area of the Sahara lying in French territory. This includes the desert portions of Algeria, as well as the neighbouring desert areas to the south, in French Equatorial Africa. This suggests that France hopes to hang on to this whole immense stretch of desert, even if some day she is driven out of the hilly coastal region of Algeria which she is now fighting so desperately to keep.

8

Inside Nowhere—the Sahara

I am never going to stand in line waiting for the first
ticket to the moon. I have already seen the moon.
That is, I have seen the fantastic mass of volcanic
rock in the middle of the Sahara known as the Hoggar. This is positively lunar in its bleak grandeur, its
quality of moon-dipped, freezing loneliness.

Even the trees, the few that exist, look like trees
you might expect to find on the moon. They are a
species of willow, greenish-white, almost like bushes
washed with silver paint—spiky, gnarled and both
brilliant and forbidding.

As for the Hoggar itself, these mountains were
formed millions of years ago when the earth of the
Sahara split, and the fires beneath the desert vomit-
ed up a few hundred million tons of earth. The lava
spurted up and then, so to speak, froze. Hence,
today, the Hoggar's separate peaks rise like scattered
puff-balls, solitary and individual; they do not form
part of a range. They look like frightful accidents of
nature—like the mushroom clouds that shoot out of
the atomic bomb.

During the day the sun eats up all their colour, but at dawn and sunset the mountains are radiantly painted with reddish-yellow, slate-blue, purple, coral and above all crimson-rose. At night, the stars hang down, just overhead, like enormous silver cherries.

I had always been told that the Sahara was flat, hot and full of sand. In the Hoggar it is about as flat as Switzerland and, in winter, as cold as ice. As for sand, I travelled into the Sahara for several days before I saw any at all, but when I did see some there was plenty. And I saw mirages—genuine mirages—all the time.

The Sahara is, of course, an area so vast that it is impossible to describe it in a word. There are oases in the Sahara green with a million date palms and moist as wet blotters. There are other sections so blindingly hot and dry that they have never been crossed by man. In Arabic the word "Sahara" means "emptiness" or "nothing."

FLIGHT TO THE HOGGAR

I flew to Tamanrasset, chief town of the Hoggar, from Algiers. The 'plane goes once a week, and the service is a long, long way from the kind of flying familiar to us of the western world. The 'plane itself was old, and the roof was painted white—for two good reasons. White deflects the hot rays of the sun, and white is also the easiest colour to see in the desert. An air-borne search party can spot a downed 'plane most easily if it is painted white. (The tops of buses and automobiles traversing the desert regularly are white for the same reason.)

We left Algiers at 4.45 on a winter morning bristling with wind and rain. Half the 'plane's space was filled with cargo, strapped by thongs to the naked sides of the fuselage and the carpetless metal floor. A 'plane on this route, which is the lifeline of the western Sahara, flies from oasis to oasis almost like a golf ball hopping from green to green.

At El Goléa, our first stop, two hours after the take-off in Algiers, the sun was burning a big yellow hole on the horizon, but it was so cold that my hands were numb. We came down on a marked strip of sand—Sahara airports have no runways in our sense —and I watched the haphazard routine of unloading which was repeated at each of our stops that day.

The weekly arrival of the 'plane from the coast was a big event. Sleepy-looking Arabs, lying about in their burnooses, as inert as logs, looked at us curiously. French soldiers gathered to gossip with our crew, while a bundle of newspapers, a crate of tomatoes, a cask of butter, were handed down into waiting arms.

Some of these soldiers were Zouaves, who are very colourful. The word "Zouave," coming from a Berber root, was first given to a body of Algerian infantrymen in the French service, famous for their dash and their brilliant uniforms. The Zouaves loitering around the El Goléa airstrip wore the round, flat-topped blue military caps called kepis, baggy black pantaloons and native sandals—

scarlet, gold, magenta or pale blue—with their toes sticking out.

There were two more stops after El Goléa, at Adrar and Alouef, lonely spots both, before we reached our destination—Tamanrasset—late that afternoon.

THE SILENT CITY OF TAMANRASSET

Tamanrasset lies almost in the centre of the world's largest desert, and the instant I stepped out of the 'plane I felt swallowed up by the Saharan void. I have never known any place so startlingly silent. If a leaf falls, it sounds like a firework. The remoteness is immeasurable.

The guest house where I stayed was an ochre-red building made of baked mud, like an adobe structure in New Mexico, but with the colour more intense. Most buildings are designed to withstand summer heat, with thick walls and small windows. They have no fireplaces or other sources of heat— wood is more precious than platinum in the desert —and in winter they are icy cold. On their outer walls are latticed designs, made of mud and shaped like paper patterns cut out by a small child. The long shallow scoops on the adobe surfaces are marks of the fingers that smoothed the mud into place.

These mud houses are apt to melt down if it rains, and vicious storms can visit this area in the autumn, although Tamanrasset once had seven solid years without a single rainfall. The town lies at an altitude of almost a mile, and in August the shade temperature can reach 126 degrees. While I was there it was only moderately hot by day, but freezing cold at night. Life in Tamanrasset goes by zigzags. The thermometer can actually drop sixty degrees between noon and night.

Tamanrasset is the capital of one of the Southern Territories of Algeria. Its population is about two thousand and it has only one street, no bank, no newspaper, no plumbing, no telephones, and electricity that works for only three hours a day, from 6 to 9 p.m. I have never seen shops as primitive as the ones here. They were like little windowless caves, so dark that it was barely possible to see the odd bits of merchandise they offered for sale—padlocks, scraps of cloth, combs.

Almost everybody I passed on the silent buff-coloured street murmured a gentle "Good day" in French. The local traders are mostly M'zabites, and there is a small Arab community composed of ex-soldiers. The bulk of the population is Negro.

These Negroes were, until fairly recently, slaves, and some would like to be slaves again, because it was easier to work as a servant for nothing than to break rock on the roads for wages. In fact, when the French administration freed the slaves, many refused to leave their masters. The Arabs get along with the Negroes quite well, but despise them. I sent an Arab boy on an errand, and offered him a small tip. He refused it proudly with the words, "Do you think I am a Negro?"

The town has one local inn, vividly French, and—a few yards away—a fondouk, the native hostel where men sleep in the courtyard beside their camels.

There are some remarkable sights in and near Tamanrasset. One is Mount Laperrine, which is only about 1,100 feet high, but dangerous and difficult to climb. Lumps of lava often break off its steep walls. This savage red mountain is named for a French general who knew the Sahara well, but who died of thirst and injuries when his aeroplane crashed in the arid wilderness near here in 1920. (Tamanrasset used to be called Fort Laperrine, and still appears by this name on some maps.)

Another famous sight is the *bordj*, or shelter, where the celebrated Père de Foucauld lived. Charles de Foucauld was one of the real heroes of French Africa. As a young army officer he was reckless and undisciplined. His family was in despair about him. Suddenly he retired alone into the desert, and founded a religious order called the Petits Frères du Sacré Coeur—the Little Brothers of the Sacred Heart. For years he taught and worked among the Tuareg, becoming their trusted adviser and spending his personal fortune on things they lacked, from needles to medicine. Père de Foucauld was killed in 1916 during an outbreak of tribal warfare. The order he founded still exists today, although its membership is not large.

THE BLUE-VEILED TUAREG

Near Tamanrasset live clusters of the Tuareg, who are among the most fascinating people in all Africa.

Tamanrasset is, in fact, their capital, insofar as these desert nomads, always on the move, have a capital.

One reason why Tuareg are so striking is that it is the men, not the women, who wear veils. The veils are of a magnificent deep blue, dyed by indigo. The colour smudges, like carbon paper, so that the men's skins often turn blue too. And they paint rings of blue paint around their eyes. In their white hoods, blue veils and blue robes, these tall, handsome men look like armoured, helmeted creatures out of science fiction—like blue bullets with blunt white tips.

I couldn't get a definite answer to my question as to why these men wear veils. Perhaps, originally, it was to hide battle wounds, because these are proud people, or simply to protect their faces from the merciless sun. Ask a Targui about this (the word "Targui" is used for one man, "Tuareg" for more than one), and the usual answer is that the custom is so old that no one remembers how it came about.

Tuareg remain veiled all the time, even inside their tents, even while eating and drinking. I never saw a male Tuareg face. It is said that if a Targui falls in battle, and his veil is swept off, his friends must veil his face again before they can decide who he is: without his usual veil he looks like a complete stranger even to his closest associates.

No one knows much about the origin of these people, but they are probably descendants of ancient Berbers. They differ from all other Berbers, however, in one striking way: they have a written language, called Tamachek. Its characters are strange looking, and vowels do not exist. This is the way my name is written in Tamachek:

ꊝI   ꊶI+:
J N   G N T R

There are two distinct classes among Tuareg—nobles and vassals. The chief distinguishing mark of the nobles is that they do no work, and until the French came to the Sahara they were headstrong warriors, camel raiders and slave traders. The vassals do all the work in a Tuareg camp, and no vassal may ever rise to become a noble.

But even Tuareg nobles are, today, poor and frugal. They live on their herds of sheep and camels, travelling from pasture to pasture. When they need money they go into the nearest town and sell a camel to the butcher. The basis of their diet is camel's milk and a kind of fine meal, or cereal, called farina. They eat with spoons—not with fingers, as Arabs do—and are remarkably clean, healthy and law-abiding.

Their swords, incidentally, look as if they might have been carried by Crusaders during the Middle Ages. This gives rise to the theory that the Tuareg may be descendants of Crusader knights who fled into the desert and intermarried with Berbers. I saw a few of these swords for sale at Tamanrasset. But I saw none of the famous Tuareg shields, made of taut antelope skins. These have become very rare since the Tuareg gave up fighting and raiding as a way of life.

I was taken out to visit some Tuareg by one of the world's foremost authorities on these people, a man named Claude Blanquernon. This Frenchman, as solid and splendid a person as anybody I ever met, was the schoolmaster in Tamanrasset when he invented "nomad schools" for the Sahara. Determined to get education out into the tribes, he travelled with one Tuareg group for a whole school year—a one-man school on camel-back, teaching the Tuareg children as the tribe moved its herds from camp to camp. The system was so successful that three other young Frenchmen took on similar jobs in the Hoggar area, where this novel method of education is now firmly entrenched.

By luck a detachment of Tuareg nobles was camped near Tamanrasset when I was there, and we set out to visit them in an open truck. With us were two Tuareg nobles who had come into town, and who volunteered to show us the way. They sent their camels back to the camp led by a vassal, but kept with them in our truck their handsome saddles which had pommels shaped like giant sword hilts.

Those Tuareg had never seen an American before, but they told us they had heard of New York. They knew that it had no camels and was beyond the sea, and that it was a large city, as large as El Goléa! (This town, with a population of about ten thousand, was the largest place they could imagine!)

For a time we drove over a hard crust of gravel, along one of the unpaved Saharan roads which are called *pistes*. Then we left the *piste* and bumped over red granite rocks and clumps of *talha*, which is a thorny variety of the yellow-flowered mimosa plant. We knew we were getting somewhere when we saw a few goats. Then, suddenly, a breath-taking line of white camels stood profiled against a rim of ruddy hill, just in front of us. We had reached the Tuareg encampment.

The ceremonial tent, where we were greeted, was made of copper-coloured leather, stretched flat between poles. A red rug covered the ground beneath this canopy. We sat down on it, cross-legged, while our hosts laboriously made a fire, out of scraps and twigs, to boil water for tea.

The ladies, unveiled, in blue robes, sat back out of the group at first, like shy frightened birds. But soon, unable to resist their curiosity, they came forward. The old leather waistcoat I happened to be wearing, which closed with a zipper, was an object of amazed fascination to the men. One by one, each nobleman made the zipper work, and they kept patting the leather, as if no leather so pliable had ever been seen before.

First we had camel's milk, which is creamy and delicious, served to all from a common bowl, to which each person put his lips. Then came the tea, poured in a stream from a tiny pot held high above the cups. It was strong and sweet and had taken a long time to prepare because the fire was so puny. Ceremoniously we drank the three cupfuls which guests in almost every part of North Africa are given. A guest who takes only one or two cups of tea (or coffee, if that is the beverage of the locality) is believed to be insulting his hosts; if he takes more than three he is greedy.

What did the Tuareg talk about, as our school-teacher-host translated? Mostly about the same things a farmer in Somerset might talk about, or a shepherd in the Welsh hills—crops, prices, the weather, local gossip.

A few weeks earlier Blanquernon had gone out into the desert and made a tape recording of the voice of the tribe's elected king, called the Aménocal. The Aménocal had asked him how much the machine cost, and had been horrified to learn it was worth four camels. As we sat drinking our tea, the story of the Aménocal and the machine was repeated to us with great relish.

Then one of our hosts told our fortunes by drawing quick, delicate designs in the sand with his fingers. I offered everybody cigarettes, and the men accepted them but put them carefully aside. They do not smoke, eat or take money in front of women.

When we left we gave one of the ladies a lift to the vassals' camp a few miles away. It was the first time in her life she had ever been in a car.

ACROSS THE SAHARA BY CAR

Having reached Tamanrasset by 'plane, I decided to return by car as far as El Goléa, the great oasis to the north.

An expedition by automobile across the Sahara is very interesting. As a rule there are regulations to fulfil and precautions to take, even for the easy route I had chosen. This was on one of two rough roads— they could not possibly be called highways in our sense—that cross the Sahara from north to south. In all the vast breadth of the Sahara, these are the only two north-south roads. And there are no east-west roads at all.

Anybody crossing the desert in his own vehicle must notify the authorities of the route he intends to follow. These authorities, officials of the Service Saharien, then send word ahead by radio (there is no telegraph) to the various towns the traveller will pass—and if the traveller doesn't reach one of those towns on schedule, a rescue car will be sent out to look for him.

In order to cover the expenses of the rescue car, the traveller must leave a deposit of money with the authorities before he sets out. The money will be returned to him if the rescue car is not needed.

The list of items which every traveller is required to carry, in addition to food and water, includes shovels, wire netting, pails and rope. The shovels may be needed to dig the car out of the sand, and the wire netting will aid in that process: it can be pushed under the wheels, in order to keep them from sinking deeper into the soft sand that has trapped them. The pails and rope may enable the traveller to obtain water from a well, if his own supply gives out. The rope should be a long one. People have died of thirst on the brink of a well, because they couldn't lower a pail deep enough into it to reach the water level.

Natives are likely to be somewhat careless about taking these precautions, now that car travel has become more common in the Sahara. They think that if they run out of water, or get lost because drifts of sand have covered the unmarked track, they will be rescued sooner or later by a car. Sometimes rescuers do come along. But sometimes not.

Few Europeans ever get lost in this part of the desert today, however, because of the strict precautions they are now required to take. Still, an Englishman did die on the road south from Tamanrasset the winter before I was there.

The French say that in summer, without water, a man lost in this region cannot expect to live more than twelve or fourteen hours. A full day in full sun will kill him. American Air Force authorities, who have made careful surveys of desert conditions for the benefit of crashed fliers, are more optimistic. Here are a few of their conclusions:

> In very hot weather, at a temperature of 100 degrees or more, a man with no water at all can survive from two to five days if he rests in the shade at all times; if he rests in the shade during the day and tries to travel at night, he will live from one to three days. If he has a quart of water he may survive half a day longer.
>
> In less hot weather, at a temperature between 80 and 100 degrees, a man with no water at all can survive from five to nine days if he rests in the shade at all times; if he rests in the shade during the day and tries to travel at night, he will live from three to seven days. If he has a quart of water he may survive half a day longer.

The word "shade" in these statements is the catch. I saw stretches of the Sahara a hundred miles long without a single speck of shade.

Dying of thirst is a painful business. A Belgian diplomat, who once almost died in the desert, told me how he had felt at the time. He said what he remembered most was that his tongue became so swollen that he could not speak, and his lips split. For weeks after he was rescued, he said, he was thirsty all the time.

My own trip overland through the desert was very picturesque but not in the least dangerous. I was lucky. I was travelling in the winter, and two French soldiers were our guides. We used a military vehicle called a *savanne*, a tough, squat, high-bodied car that can go anywhere over sand or rocks like a rabbit. The unpaved *piste* wasn't too bad. Usually it was simply a wide track, or stony belt, which looked very much like the surrounding desert. I've known worse roads in Scotland or Vermont—though I never before travelled on such a bad road for three days on end. It took us three days of hard driving to cover the 730 miles from Tamanrasset to El Goléa.

Here are a few notes on each day's travel:

First day, Tamanrasset to Arak: We drove eleven hours and never once saw any other vehicle in all that time except one bus. It was en route all the way across the Sahara, from Fort Lamy in French Equatorial Africa to Algiers on the Mediterranean coast. When we overtook it, it was already twelve *days* late, because of the many breakdowns it had had. Near the spot where we saw the bus we also saw a cluster of blanched camel skeletons—grisly reminders of caravan animals that had died some time in the past.

We saw only one sign of habitation during the entire day, a cluster of Arab huts. There was not a single petrol pump in the whole distance of about 235 miles. But there were occasional signs to indicate wells, and at one point we crossed the Tropic of Cancer, neatly marked.

We travelled through the Hoggar a great part of the time, past mountains that looked like elephants, like swollen gourds, like crushed duffel bags. Our car crawled and slid like a lizard among rocks that had fallen on to the *piste*. Every few minutes our chauffeur stopped abruptly, lifted up his carbine and tried to shoot one of the gazelles visible in the distance. "A near miss!" he growled several times, but he never got one.

Motor cars have been travelling over the Sahara only since the 1920's. Before then the only way to cross it was by camel. In those days the desert was measured in terms of a day's travel by camel, and it was said to be "seven months wide by four months deep." Our one-day trip from Tamanrasset to Arak would have taken between two and three weeks by camel.

Arak, our destination that night, is not a town. It is simply a *bordj*, or shelter, built there because the regulations provide that there must be a shelter every 250 miles along this road. Nothing else exists there, nothing whatsoever. Our host, who may see a European every two weeks or so, gave us an extraordinarily good dinner (the two main courses were potatoes). He also told us about the rock paintings which have been found in this part of the Sahara— paintings which suggest that once the desert here was greener and less arid that it is now, and supported a group of primitive people who lived on game.

Second day, Arak to In Salah: All signs of vegetation ceased soon after we started out. Before this there had been isolated patches of desert scrub, enough for goats to feed on. But now we passed through a barren wilderness of nothing at all but stones. In the distance slopes of white sand, looking like snowbanks, lay at the foot of the red mountains.

At noon we spread blankets out on the rough black gravel and had a picnic. To my amazement a living thing appeared—a fly.

In the afternoon the *piste* improved. It didn't meander so much, and we no longer had the sense of driving in an endless dry river bed. Mileposts were neater and closer together (they were kilometre posts really, because measurements are in kilometres here). Even so we didn't pass a single car all day. Nor did we see any sign of human beings at all until we passed the camp of some oil prospectors not far from our destination, the town of In Salah, about 170 miles from our starting point at the Arak shelter.

The oasis of In Salah has a population of five thousand natives, mostly Negro, and forty-three French. Mud prickles adorn the orange-coloured buildings, and the familiar latticed pattern appeared on gates and walls. This oasis is much less picturesque than Tamanrasset, and closer to Europe in some ways. There is electric light, for example, until 10 p.m. every night! But the sook (market) was the emptiest and most forlorn I ever visited. Flies clung to children like lumps of liquorice.

The oasis of In Salah supports eighty thousand date palm trees, and this is perhaps a good place to say a word about oases. Usually they are found at low places in the terrain, at spots where water collects underground after creeping invisibly through sand and rock. If underground water exists close enough to the surface to feed the roots of date palms, the place will probably become the green, shady location we know as an oasis. But elaborate engineering is usually necessary to make irrigation channels, tap springs and bring the water to the trees. In a well-tended oasis there are, so to speak, three levels of vegetation: dates towering above, citrus and other fruit trees planted in their shade below and vegetables and flowers close to the ground. Each oasis is a heart, and the water pumped into its groves is the lifeblood of the Sahara.

Third day, In Salah to El Goléa: For two hours after we left In Salah in the morning of our third day, we saw nothing, not even a scrap of bush. The desert here is black, not yellow. The very rocks are sun-burned to a black tone. We reached the great Tade-maït Plateau, and climbed it almost as one would climb a flight of stairs. At the top we saw a long camel caravan, marching slowly against the sky. It looked so much like caravans in movies that it was hard to believe it was real.

At noon we reached an oil camp in Fort Miribel, where we saw a sign post that read: Bidon Cinq, 1,379 kilometres; Tombouctou (Timbuktu), 2,293 kilometres; Fort Lamy, 3,907 kilometres.

Bidon Cinq, a French name which means "can five," is a fuel dump established for the use of travellers on the other north-south road through the Sahara. Originally there were other such dumps called Can One, Can Two and so forth. But now that cars need refuelling less often only Bidon Cinq remains.

Timbuktu, of course, is the almost legendary city, sought by so many explorers, on the southern edge of the great desert. The first European to reach the place, and return to tell of his adventures, was young René Caillié, a French orphan who dreamed of finding Timbuktu from the time he was a child, and who finally accomplished his goal in 1828. For centuries before this it had been an important native capital.

We had lunch at the camp of Dutch oil prospectors working in the neighbourhood of Fort Miribel. Many Frenchmen who love the Sahara hope that the search for oil will fail. "For twenty years," one officer told me, "we have been trying to teach the natives to grow crops, to develop a satisfactory agriculture, to live decently on the land. Now come the oil invaders, and everybody rushes off to work in their camps. Oil may enrich the Sahara. Also it may ruin it." The French may have made mistakes, but many individual Frenchmen are passionately devoted to their work in Africa, and want to do everything possible to improve the situation of the Africans.

When we left Fort Miribel we passed on to the brittle rocky channel between two of the most feared areas in the whole Sahara—the Great Western Emptiness and the Great Eastern Emptiness. And there, between those two solid sandy ergs, or wastes, our car had a minor breakdown—sand in the carburettor. While it was being fixed I marvelled at the mirages that stretched out on three sides of us, glittering, shimmering, brighter than silver, like shallow flat discs of mercury. The whitish stuff right alongside the *piste* was even more interesting in a way. When I walked over it, it had the feeling of foam that had been crushed solid. It was pure salt.

Our third day's trip was the longest, about three hundred miles, but it ended at one of the most wonderful oases in the Sahara, El Goléa. Our 'plane had put down here on the way south, and now I had returned. This time I had the chance to explore the city, from headquarters in a comfortable hotel.

El Goléa is so hot during the summer that even 'plane traffic stops. But it is beautiful in autumn and spring, and when I was there—in the winter—it was delightful by day but cold enough at night. We appreciated the big fire made of rough palm fronds that helped heat the hotel, and we used metal hot-water bottles when we went to bed.

I waded around in the sand dunes that slide massively in on the oasis from the big ergs on either side. Those dunes take on every colour—amber, fawn, white—as the vibrating sunlight changes. And the sand is so soft and fine that you can sink into it up to your knees. When the winds blow along the ridges of these formidable smooth dunes, and lift plumes of sand from their tops, the natives say that the sand is "smoking."

Water spurts out of the ground all the year round here—good water, fit to drink—and it makes an excellent place for date palms, which must have hot sun and plenty of water. When the French came to El Goléa there were only six thousand palms in the oasis; today there are well over a hundred thousand. About sixty trees will support a single family. Many

acres of the big date groves here are owned by
French people, who buy a stand of the palms as an
investment, the way Americans buy real estate in
Florida. Few French actually live here, however.
The ten thousand inhabitants are mostly Arabs and
a variety of Berber known as Zenetes.

The great sight of El Goléa is the slate-coloured
Vieux Ksar, or Old Fort, dominating a bleak hill
nearby. It has been there for nine hundred years. A
Swiss engineer was asked recently if any modern
architect could build such a structure, out of mud,
without steel, without nails, without cement, and
hope to have it last that long. His answer was a
definite "No."

I spent an afternoon here with the White Fathers,
a Catholic order founded in 1847 with the purpose
of Christianizing Moslems in Africa. Its members,
who wear beards and immaculate white robes, have
done much good work for education all over the
continent. In El Goléa there is a school run by their
associates, the White Sisters. The White Fathers say
now that they no longer make much of an attempt
to convert Moslems to Christianity. They say that
—in this region, at least—this is almost impossible.
One White Father told me, "The Moslems here do
not *bend*, either to the forces of reason or of history."

At the El Goléa hospital the resident doctor told
me that in ten years he has never had a case of
appendicitis in a native, or seen a cancer. I asked
him about tuberculosis. "None as yet in the Sahara,"
he said. But he added that it might some day be
brought into the desert by settlers from Europe or
other areas where tuberculosis is common.

CAMELS

Camels are odd beasts—so slow, so stately and so haughty. Camels and their masters never show affection for each other, as horses and their masters do, for example. Camel owners don't even name their beasts very often. And I never came across anybody who said that a camel recognized a human being, even a man who had been riding the animal for months.

A good riding camel costs £30 to £35, a baggage camel about £20. But most people don't buy camels—they raise them. An animal is adult at seven years, and can usually work until he is about fifteen years old. The favoured colour for a smart riding animal is a pale, pinkish, eggshell shade called *azrem*.

Normally camels can cover fifteen miles a day. In cool weather particularly good animals might make as much as twenty-five. They always travel by soft ground, if possible, never on the stony *pistes*, because hard ground splits their hooves. Their worst enemy is mud. In winter they can go literally for months without water, if they have good moist pasture and are not working. If working, camels can live without water for only ten or twelve days even with good pasture, and for no more than five or six days with poor pasture. In summer, no matter what kind of pasture they get, they must be watered every other day.

Generally you can tell the state of a camel's health by the hardness of his hump. If he is overworked or underfed (camels eat a lot), the hump shrinks; if he is put to good pasture, the hump will grow again if the beast is not too old. But usually, if a camel is tired or sick, he doesn't show any signs of it. He simply collapses and dies suddenly, without any warning at all.

If you see a cluster of two or three camels travelling across the desert, you know it is a family on the move. A real camel caravan, carrying goods for trading purposes, usually averages about forty to fifty animals—although there may be as few as six camels in a caravan or as many as two hundred. The Arabs who lead caravans seem to find their way across the trackless desert by some superhuman instinct. They will remember a basic dune pattern even when half of it has been blown away.

I asked if camels would ever be replaced by that marvellously efficient vehicle, the jeep. The answer was no, for at least three reasons. First, petrol costs money. Second, even a jeep can't cross the great empty ergs. Third, you can't eat a jeep if it dies.

9

Libya: A Youthful Nation
Learning Its Way

THIS little-known country, Libya, is packed with
curiosities. Few foreigners—even if they know where
it is—appreciate its vastness. It is bigger than all
western Europe, and one-fifth the size of the entire
United States.

It fronts on the Mediterranean, and projects deep
into the Sahara. It has no rivers, and is almost completely arid, except for a few oases. It can rain cats
and dogs along the coast—as I will freely attest—
but it has practically no fresh water except well
water in the lonely oases.

A famous wind, called the *ghibli*, is locally regarded as the most unpleasant wind in the world.
Blowing northward from the Sahara, it sprays
brown sand over the coastal towns, and brings the
heat on occasion to 120 degrees.

The hottest shade temperature ever known, 136.4
degrees, was recorded in the Libyan desert only a
few miles south of the coastal city of Tripoli.

No valuable minerals have been found in Libya, and no oil—although it is always possible that such resources may be discovered in the future. (After all, Saudi Arabia was once considered "worthless," and it has become fabulously rich since oil was located beneath its barren desert.) Only 2 per cent of the land is productive. So Libya is one of the poorest nations in the world.

The total population is only about 1,150,000, which is comparable with that of Birmingham. But the country finds it difficult to provide a decent living even for this small number. The average income probably doesn't exceed £12 per person per year.

Libya has no bank of its own. It has no native doctor of medicine. There are not more than 225 miles of railway. Some of its shortcomings may be remedied in the fairly near future, however. After all, Libya is still one of the youngest countries in the world—only a few years older than independent Morocco and Tunisia.

Libya did not fight for its independence, in the way those two countries had to do. Formerly an Italian colony, it was given its life as a free nation on December 24, 1951, by the United Nations—the first nation ever put on its feet, such as they are, by the UN. So it is still a child learning to walk, under the watchful eye of its foster parents. And no one can be sure how it will develop and mature.

Poverty is obviously one of Libya's greatest problems. But another problem, equally serious, results from the fact that this "box of sand" is not really one country, but three—three separate "nations" which were combined to make the United Kingdom of Libya.

Those three subdivisions of the new country—Tripolitania, Cyrenaica and Fezzan—all have their own special history and background. Persuading them to work together now, as a single smoothly operating unit, is not an easy task.

Tripolitania and Cyrenaica, for example, lie side by side along the coast, and have the same climate and geography, but they are different in almost every other way. There is not much communication between the two, even now, and the people of each dislike and mistrust each other.

TRIPOLITANIA AND ITS ROMANTIC HISTORY

Tripolitania has a population of about eight hundred thousand—more than half the population of the United Kingdom of Libya. It lies in the western end of the new Libyan nation and shares, for the most part, the history of its neighbour, Tunisia. Like Tunisia, it was first invaded by the Phoenicians, then occupied by Rome, next overrun by the Vandals and afterward occupied by the Romans again.

Tripolitania produced one of its greatest heroes during the first period of Roman occupation. He was a Berber with African Negro blood, a warrior named Septimius Severus. As a trusted general in the Roman army Severus received word, one day, that the Emperor of Rome had been assassinated, and he promptly set out to avenge the death. When he had accomplished this purpose and the murderer had been punished, Severus himself was proclaimed Emperor of Rome. He was the only African ever to achieve this position, and he brought great glory to his homeland. He ruled from A.D. 193 to 211, conducted victorious forays into Mesopotamia and Europe and died in—of all places—York.

The Romans built a famous group of cities along the Tripolitanian coast. They were usually called the "Three Towns," and their names were Sabratha, Leptis Magna and Oea. Today some of the most magnificent Roman ruins in all Africa may be seen at Sabratha and Leptis Magna, where archaeologists have worked laboriously to dig away the sands of centuries. At Leptis Magna whole streets have been uncovered, paved with heavy stones that still bear the mark of Roman chariot wheels. At Sabratha the golden columns of a Roman theatre, glowing in the sun, rise dramatically against the blue backdrop of the Mediterranean.

Of these "Three Towns" only Oea is alive today, under the newer name of Tripoli. The name "Tripoli" means "three towns," and it originally designated all three of the ancient Roman settlements. Tripoli has been the capital of Tripolitania for a long time and is still its most important city. For hundreds of years the history of the country was chiefly the history of this colourful port.

After the Arab conquest of North Africa, in the eighth century, Tripoli became an important trade centre and a prize captured and recaptured by

7

various warring Moslem sects. Once it was seized by a clever ruse. A seemingly innocent camel caravan went through the gates, its heavily laden beasts each bearing two big sacks. When the caravan reached the central square, those sacks suddenly burst open, and out of each one tumbled an armed man. The amazed bystanders were too startled to defend themselves. The city fell quickly, almost without bloodshed.

The second invasion of Arabs—the wild tribes sent out of Egypt to ravage North Africa in the eleventh century—broke Tripoli's spirit. But it remained a beautiful city, with dazzling white houses and green gardens, and kept up a thriving trade. Its rulers exerted little authority, however, over the rest of the sandy countryside, and they had little influence over their neighbour capitals. During the following centuries Tripolitania was generally regarded as the weakest of all the North African states. For a long time it was under Turkish rule.

In the year 1714—in the heyday of Tripoli's pirate period—there occurred one of the most terrible nights in the city's history. It made Tripolitania independent again, but it certainly didn't bring her people true freedom. The hero—or villain —of the occasion was an ambitious Turkish official named Ahmed Caramanli, who had made up his mind to achieve both power and wealth. He won them both on that one night, and by a simple but effective trick.

Caramanli laid the groundwork for his plot by inviting to dinner the three hundred most important officers of the Turkish garrison. Then, that night, he posted servants in the niches along the dark corridor, or alleyway, that led from the street to the main rooms of his palace. The guests arrived on schedule. One by one they started down the corridor, were seized by Caramanli's hidden servants, dragged inside and murdered. Not a single guest survived. Before the evening was over Caramanli was the only Turkish authority left in Tripoli, and he had no opposition when he declared himself to be Hamet the Great, ruler of all Tripolitania.

Cruel, ruthless and autocratic, the Caramanli clan bled the country white and ran the piracy business as a kind of family monopoly.

The castle where the Caramanlis lived for over a hundred years still stands in Tripoli today, its crumbling amber walls facing out to sea. Its cellars are still damp, as they were in the days when Christian slaves were chained to the walls and floors. And if you visit some of its empty upper rooms, your guide may show you one, at least, with a dark history. Here Hamet the Great's great-grandson murdered his own brother in order to gain the throne.

As we know, Tripoli was forced to sign a no-piracy treaty with the United States in 1815, but Tripolitanian raiders continued to seize ships of other countries. The Caramanli clan grew steadily richer, as the people of Tripolitania grew poorer and more miserable under its rule. On the whole it seemed like a change for the better when Turkey overthrew the Caramanlis in 1835 and made Tripolitania a Turkish province once more.

This time the Turks kept a firm grip on the country. Few foreigners were allowed to enter, because the Turkish sultan suspected all foreigners of being spies. And the Berber villages of the interior were cut off completely from the rest of the world. Life was primitive, and the people had savage customs. When a man was about to be executed, for example, for having committed a murder, the execution was performed by the son of the murdered man—while the murdered man's widow or widows stood by in their best clothes, to watch the spectacle and to drink the dead man's blood.

In time Tripoli became run-down, as its trade steadily dwindled. Few ships put in at its port.

But the city remained a strategic spot, in which all the European powers were interested. France, England and Italy looked at it jealously. Turkey managed to hold on to its African territory for a while, but then the Italians took a hand.

THE FEZZAN—MORE SAND

The Fezzan—the desert region south of Tripoli—is still largely unknown country. It has few towns, and contains only 4 per cent of Libya's total population.

But Herodotus, the Greek historian who lived in the fifth century B.C., wrote about the Fezzan and its scattered oases. The people there were called Garamantes in those days and Herodotus described their strange cattle which, he said, had forward-bending horns, which made it difficult for them to feed. He also said that the Garamantes went on slave-hunting expeditions among the more primitive cave-dwelling people, or troglodytes, who lived nearby. They had to use horse-drawn chariots for the chase, according to the story, because the troglodytes could run much faster than ordinary men.

Herodotus wrote, too, about monstrous headless men, and men with dogs' heads, which he said inhabited the desert between the Fezzan oases and the Mediterranean coast.

The bloodthirsty Arab conqueror, Sidi Okba, rode through the Fezzan during his campaign for North Africa. Legend says that his horse, pawing the ground, laid bare the spring where the town of Gadàmes now stands, thus creating an oasis. Gadàmes, one of the oldest settlements in North Africa, became an important relay point for caravans.

The Berber inhabitants of Gadàmes today are stern, backward Moslems. The inhabitants of most of the Fezzan's other oases, strung out over several hundred miles, are chiefly Arab nomads and Negroes descended from slaves brought from the Sudan.

In the sixteenth century the Turks declared their authority over the Fezzan. But because the area is so remote, it has seldom been actually invaded. For most of its history it has been a kind of vassal state of Tripoli—a city with which it has no direct communication, even today, except by camel.

The capital, Sébha, has a population of fifty thousand. But even this sizeable town is incredibly isolated and remote. Automobile traffic and aeroplanes reach it from Tunis, not from Tripoli. Sébha has no easy road or air connections with any other part of Libya, although it is a Libyan city.

CYRENAICA AND THE SENUSSI

The history of Cyrenaica, the third of the three
countries that make up present-day Libya, is quite
different from that of the rest of North Africa. Cyrenaica was never, for example, a part of the Roman
Empire. Greeks settled here, not Romans. And it
remained under Greek influence for about twelve
hundred years—from about 600 B.C. to A.D. 600.

The Greek settlements here included Cyrene,
which gave the country its name, and Berenice, now
called Benghazi, which is now the capital of Cyrenaica. One of the loveliest statues of Venus in the
world comes from Cyrene.

Cyrene was a wealthy city in ancient times, chiefly
because a plant called silphium grew luxuriously on
the surrounding plateau. Silphium, the Greeks believed, could cure almost anything, including scor-
pion bites, dog bites, carbuncles, corns and calluses.
Mixed with "wine and saffron and pepper and mice
dung and vinegar," it was supposed to cure ulcers
too. Cyrene grew so rich on its silphium crop that
it became the first city in all Africa to issue its own
coinage—at a time when even Carthage did not
have coins.

When Alexander the Great conquered the whole
eastern end of the Mediterranean, in the fourth century B.C., and built the city of Alexandria in Egypt,
his Greek subjects in Cyrenaica suddenly found
themselves part of his vast empire. Naturally, after
that, Cyrenaicans sent to Egypt for help in time of
trouble, and several of the men of learning who
made Alexandria famous came from Cyrenaica.

Eratosthenes, head librarian of Alexandria's magnificent library, and one of the great scientists of ancient times, was born in Cyrene. Two thousand years ago—when everyone believed that the world was flat—he proved to himself, by studying the stars and the shadows cast by the sun, that it was actually round. He also proved that it was a great deal larger than people thought at the time. In fact, working out the circumference of the globe, he was wrong by only four hundred miles! If people had accepted Eratosthenes' ideas at the time, rather than waiting for some fifteen hundred years, the whole history of mankind might have been changed.

Cyrenaica became part of the Islamic empire in the eighth century, and three hundred years later Arabs from Egypt went through it with fire and sword. Then in the sixteenth century it became a Turkish province, and remained under Turkish rule until the Italians made war on Turkey in 1912.

But, meantime, a fiery and devout organization of Arabs grew up out in the desert, known as the Senussi. These Arabs were patriots and puritan reformers, and the Senussi Order has played a great role in the history of the area ever since.

The Order was founded by a man, born in Algeria in 1787, who was called the Grand Senussi. He was a member of a Bedouin tribe, and was a scholar and a mystic. Originally he planned to make his headquarters in Algeria, but when the French took over that country he came to Cyrenaica instead. There he and his first followers built their Mother Lodge near Cyrene in 1843. Local chapters of the Order—called *zawias*—soon sprang up in almost every village and oasis of the country, and had their own town halls and schools.

After the Grand Senussi's death in 1859 his two sons carried on the work, and established a university at the Kufra oasis in central Cyrenaica. Each local lodge contributed money to this university, and its students were sent out to serve as missionaries among the Bedouin. They had fanatic zeal, and the result today is that about 90 per cent of the people of Cyrenaica are Senussi.

Until 1911 the Senussi were on the whole peaceable enough. The Turkish administration, recognizing their power, worked through the local *zawias* in order to govern Cyrenaica's scattered Arab tribes. But when the Italians attacked the country, the Senussi fought back fiercely.

LIBYA AS AN ITALIAN COLONY

Italy came late to the African grab. By the time Italy got interested in Africa, there was not much left to take. She was too weak to fight the French, who had established a hold over Algeria, Tunisia and Morocco. She couldn't hope to get anywhere in Egypt, because England was already there. So all Italy could do was fight Turkey and try to conquer the three Turkish-held Libyan states in North Africa. The war she launched against Turkey was cold-blooded and ruthless.

Italy took Tripolitania and the Fezzan easily enough, and defeated the Turkish overlords of Cyrenaica too. But the Cyrenaicans themselves—that is, chiefly the Senussi—simply refused to be Italian subjects.

Two prolonged, exhausting Italo-Senussi wars took place. The first lasted from 1911 to 1917. During its last years, when the First World War was also going on, the Senussi even joined their former masters, the Turks, to fight against the Italians. And when peace was finally established, it didn't last long. The Senussi began to fight the Italians all over again in 1923, and were not defeated until 1932.

One heroic Senussi leader, Omar Al Mukhtar, held out to the last in the Kufra oasis. When the Italians finally got him they hanged him publicly—although he was gravely wounded—before an audience of twenty thousand tribesmen forced to attend the ceremony. It is an index of Senussi toughness—and patriotism—that they didn't surrender until they had lost *one-third* of their total adult male population.

The story is often told, but denied by the Italians, that during those campaigns the Italians invented a novel method of frightening their enemies: they grabbed a local sheikh, took him up in an aeroplane, identified him with a placard tied around his neck and pitched him overboard—alive—on whatever village happened to be in need of "pacification."

The Italians tried to use their new Libyan colony to draw off the surplus population of their overcrowded homeland. This policy was encouraged by every possible means, but only about ninety-two thousand Italians from the mainland actually settled in Libya.

Italy gave Libya some good public buildings and

new roads, but did practically nothing for native education or public health. There was little training for self-government. There was not even any effort —such as the French sometimes made—to assimilate the Africans into European culture. Civil rights were unknown.

Benito Mussolini, who became the Fascist dictator of Italy in 1922 and who dreamed of re-creating a Roman Africa, changed this policy to an extent in order to win Arab good will. He sought to give the Africans some economic benefits, and the standard of living rose. In fact, it was higher in Tripoli under the Italians than it is today. Many Arabs in the towns became friendly toward Italy.

But Mussolini never won any friends among the fierce, desert-dwelling Senussi. They fought their second war against Italy during his regime.

LIBYA—AN INDEPENDENT STATE AT LAST

Italy automatically lost Libya, her North African colony, when she was defeated by the Allies in 1943. But when the war was finally over the victors couldn't make up their minds what to do about Libya. While France temporarily held the Fezzan (which French forces had taken during the war, after a brilliant cross-desert march from French Equatorial Africa), and while the British took charge of the rest of the country, the United Nations discussed Libya's long-range future.

The United States delegation suggested a "collective trusteeship" under the UN, to run for ten years, after which the problem could be dealt with anew. This would probably have been the most sensible solution. For various reasons the plan fell through. Then the Russians asked for a trusteeship of their own over Tripolitania, but this proposal alarmed everybody. Then a three-way partition of Libya was suggested, with the French getting a trusteeship over the Fezzan, the British over Cyrenaica and the Italians over Tripolitania—but most UN members thought it would be fantastic to give any part of Libya back to Italy, which had just been defeated in the war.

In the end, as people got tired of wrangling, Libya's future was settled with almost indecent haste. Late in 1950 the UN decided that the country should become independent before December 31, 1951. This meant that the whole machinery of government had to be created in a little more than a year—an almost impossible job. For instance, at that time there were only seventeen Libyans in the entire country who had ever graduated from a university. Yet an administration had to be set up.

Luckily, several Britons, who had been running the country during the post-war period, agreed to stay on for a time as employees of the new Libyan government. And conscientious Libyans—and men of many other nationalities—pooled their efforts. There seemed general agreement that a constitutional monarchy would be the best form of government for the new nation. And an obvious candidate for the throne was ready. He was the leader of the Senussis, grandson of the founder of the Order.

HIS MAJESTY THE KING OF LIBYA

The full name of Libya's king, first ruler of the new country, is al-Sayyid Mohammed Idris al-Mahdi es Senussi. He is usually known simply as King Idris I.

The chief characteristics of this thoughtful, somewhat frail old gentleman—he was born in 1889—seem to be piety and suspiciousness. He has considerable nobility of character and a subtle intelligence, and believes devoutly in Libyan freedom. He knows no Western language, but is an Arabic scholar of real distinction, and is probably the most sophisticated as well as learned head of state in the Moslem world. His chief defect is lack of force.

When I saw him—not in his own country, but in Cairo, where he was recuperating from an illness—King Idris was seated in the middle of a sofa, and I faced him in a chair a few feet away. He has a bushy moustache and gold-rimmed glasses; he wore a blue cloak and a short tarboosh, or brimless hat. My first impression was that this was an extremely gentle man. He has the reputation of being even more reticent than most Arab potentates, so it was a welcome surprise to find that he talked readily—with charm and humour. Idris may be frail, but his wits are still sharp.

He talked about Morocco and about the United States, as well as about his own country. Tunisia and Morocco were not yet independent at that time, and he asked—with a gleam in his eye—why the United States worked so hard to liberate countries behind the Iron Curtain, while neglecting countries that would always be their friends, like Tunisia and Morocco.

In the familiar Moslem pattern, as old as Islam
itself, King Idris was a religious figure first—he became head of the Senussi Order in 1917—and then
turned to politics. In time he became the Emir of
Cyrenaica (*Emir* is an Arabic title that means
"chieftain") and was recognized as such by the
Italians for a brief period, until he was forced to flee
to Egypt. During the Second World War he assisted
the British greatly, and he returned to his country
in 1943. He had been in exile for twenty-one years!
In 1949 the British made him Emir of Cyrenaica
again, while waiting for a final UN decision on
Libya as a whole. Then a national assembly
proclaimed him King of Libya.

Idris has no male heir, and has named his jovial,
socially minded brother, Rida, as his Crown Prince.
Rida and Idris' Queen, Fatima (who of course is
never seen), are, curiously enough, the only members
of the large royal family who are not in exile. The
reason for this was an event that took place in 1954,
an event sensational even for an oriental monarchy.

In October of that year the Minister of Palace
Affairs was murdered by one of the King's nephews.
It was well known that many members of the Idris
family—including no fewer than thirty-eight royal
princes—were opposed to some of his policies. But
for one of his own relatives to assassinate his own
chief minister was too much. So Idris exiled all of
the princes except his brother—packed them off to
a forlorn oasis in the middle of the desert—to teach
them a lesson. The nineteen-year-old prince who
committed the murder was executed, even though
he was of royal blood.

The chief problem of Libya is the division of opinion that still exists among its various parts, and especially between Tripolitania and Cyrenaica.

Many people in Tripolitania speak of Idris scornfully as a "shepherd chieftain" who was "foisted" on them. They say that he favours Cyrenaica against the interests of the rest of the country. For instance, Idris refuses to live in Tripoli, although the Senate and the House of Representatives meet there. He sends Crown Prince Rida to Tripoli, as Deputy King, while he himself spends most of his time in a palace near Benghazi, or at his summer capital in the hilly region of Cyrenaica.

It does seem to be true that Idris likes Benghazi better than Tripoli, although the two cities are joint capitals. This is just one aspect of the fact that Libya is not yet, by any means, a truly united nation.

LIBYA'S PLACE IN THE WORLD

In 1953 Libya officially allied herself with Egypt, and her other neighbours to the east, by joining the Arab League, the militant bloc that stimulates and encourages Arab nationalism everywhere. Egypt, its leader, has always wanted to create a close tie with Libya as well as all other Arab states.

But the Arab League—particularly since the rise of Colonel Nasser, Egypt's military dictator, and the Suez crisis in October, 1956—has steadily tended to become more anti-Western and pro-Soviet. The Libyans, even though they are Arabs, don't like this, since in general they want good, close relations with Great Britain and the United States.

Libya needs, above all, money and skills, and this fact controls—or should control—her policy. "Get some food into our bellies, get some knowledge into our heads," one elderly Libyan official told me when I asked him what his countrymen needed most. And most Libyans realize that they are likely to get more of the kind of help they need from the West than from Egypt. Besides, they are strongly anti-Communist, and don't want to be anybody's puppet.

Libya has willingly signed treaties with both England and the United States. In exchange for British financial help, the British are allowed to keep certain forces inside Libya. And the United States maintains an important air installation there, Wheelus Field. Also Americans are giving Libya a tremendous lot of technical and financial aid.

Wheelus Field, situated near Tripoli, is not, technically speaking, a "base," but is merely a "field," an essential stopping place for U.S. military 'planes flying around the globe, and a gunnery practice site. Even in far-off Africa, such sites are needed.

Originally the U.S. government leased the land for this big field—its runway is eleven thousand feet long—from fourteen hundred different Libyan property owners. Several years later, in 1954, it signed an agreement by which the U.S. will pay Libya forty-five million dollars over a period of twenty years, and give the country other economic aid as well, in exchange for the use of Wheelus Field.

LOOKING TOWARD LIBYA'S FUTURE

American and UN advisers, working together, have turned Libya into something like a school. They are instructing almost its whole population, directly or indirectly, trying to keep the country on its feet and teach it to walk. No doubt there has been extravagance in the programme and mistakes may have been made, but even so this work is doing good far beyond its cost.

This U.S.-UN programme operates in four major fields: public health, natural resources, agriculture and education. All sorts of experts, from many different countries, have come to carry out the work —including specialists in such varied fields as taxation, animal hides and skins, forestry, date palms, child psychology and manual training.

In public health the major problem is trachoma, the terrible eye disease that afflicts—or has afflicted —about 90 per cent of all Libyan children. Flies spread this disease, and teams of men are patiently teaching people how to use DDT to keep down flies. If trachoma is arrested in time, blindness will not result.

As to natural resources and agriculture, the main effort is to increase food crops. The U.S. sent a big shipment of wheat here in 1953, when a serious drought almost caused a famine. But in the Fezzan people get only about eight hundred food calories a day even during years of normal rainfall—which means they live close to starvation all the time. A long-range programme is necessary to meet this situation. American experts have been surveying the desert, mapping underground water sources and trying to improve crop quality. Education is the best hope, although it has been difficult so far to persuade farmers to learn new agricultural methods.

Esparto grass, used for making fine paper, is one of Libya's few distinctive products, and efforts are being made to increase production of this. Native wool is also being improved. Sheep-owners are being taught, for example, to clean out the "dung tags" which keep their wool out of a high-priced market, and the value of Libyan wool has increased substantially as a result. Thousands of seedling trees have also been planted, in a programme with the elaborate name of "sand dune stabilization project." This may eventually lead to an increase in the amount of usable land in the country.

One curious difficulty that visiting experts have encountered is the devotion of Libyans to their donkeys. Donkey dung can be used as a fuel, and donkeys turn the water wheels, but otherwise the animals are useless. They don't give milk, meat, leather, wool and transportation, as camels do. This is why the experts would like to see camels used instead. But Libyans are used to donkeys and don't want to give them up.

Education is a whole long story in itself. Like practically every other new country in Africa, Libya is education-mad. "The thirst for education is like that of a man trying to suck water out of sand," one UN official told me. When the country became independent only about 10 per cent of the population could read and write, but plans for compulsory education were made immediately, with the help of the member nations of the UN, and progress is already noticeable.

Now, out in the oases, schools operate in three shifts. Communities even volunteer to create their own schools, so that they won't have to wait until the government does it for them. But Libya is poor and the schools are miserably equipped. A blackboard—even a pencil—is a rare and expensive object. Also, because of the Moslem attitude to women, it is hard to give education to girls. Arabs don't want their daughters to go to school, and the ratio of boy students to girls in Libya is still about a hundred to one.

But there are hopeful signs. The winds of the modern world are blowing—even here. In Benghazi a well-born Moslem girl, only sixteen years old, told her family that she was leaving home to become a teacher, because it humiliated her that almost all Cyrenaican schoolteachers had to be men imported from Syria or Egypt. Teacher-training is still one of Libya's prime needs. Another is training in skilled trades, like carpentry.

The U.S. Information Service has done some good work here. It presents films, mostly on American subjects—films that are so popular they have to be shown in shifts and libraries in Tripoli and Benghazi are thronged. People who can read at all seem to want to read any book, on any subject, and there aren't enough to go round. If Washington would spend even a little more money on these libraries, it could make a world of difference.

The American authorities have also distributed radios throughout the country, mostly to clubs, schools and other organizations, so that each one can reach a large audience.

THE TWO CAPITALS: TRIPOLI AND BENGHAZI

Even though Libya itself is wretchedly poor, the city of Tripoli—with a population of around 140,000 —is one of the best built, cleanest and generally most attractive cities in North Africa. Italians know how to build cities, and they spent a great deal of money here. The principal thoroughfares are broad, and the pavements are shaded by handsome arcades.

There are all sorts of reminders of Tripoli's past, too, such as ancient Roman columns mortised into five-hundred-year-old Turkish walls. And the most imposing structure in all Tripoli is still the old Castello, or fort, that once housed the Caramanli family. Just opposite it stands the Caramanli mosque, topped by glistening white minarets and cupolas, where members of the family are buried under white tombstones capped by curious little monuments. These depict white marble turbans on marble columns. One visitor thought they looked like "rows of petrified turnips."

Even the Arab quarter of Tripoli is clean, but the sooks are poorer and not as colourful as most North African markets. Among the few really picturesque things that tempt the visitor are gold necklaces, made of a multitude of chains, that spread like a big bib from a woman's throat to her waist. Dangling from the chains are tiny gold hands and golden fish. The hands are symbols of Fatima, daughter of the Prophet Mohammed, and the fish are good-luck charms.

Tripolitan women, incidentally, wear a costume known as the barracan. It is a cloak worn like a blanket, to cover the whole body and head. In public the wearer pulls the barracan over her face too, so that it also serves as a veil. She leaves just one eye exposed—the left eye.

But probably the most interesting sight in Tripoli —for Americans, at least—is the old Protestant cemetery where five American sailors lie buried. They were members of the crew of the U.S.S. *Intrepid*, which was blown up in Tripoli harbour during the Barbary wars. After an American force landed near Tripoli, and planted the Stars and Stripes there on April 27, 1804, no United States force invaded Africa again until GI's landed in 1942 during the Second World War.

From the air it is easy to see that Tripoli is an oasis. Its edges are so sharp that it looks as if the green-and-white shape had been cut out of the surrounding tawny sand with a pastry cutter. Smaller oases are also visible from a 'plane, as well as Berber villages back in the hills and the fishing towns strung out along the Italian-built highway that rims the coast.

Communication by commercial air routes is not very good in North Africa, to put it mildly. Services across Libya (or even between Tunis and Tripoli) are scant. Maybe there will be a 'plane once a week —maybe not. A British company decided to open a Libyan air service recently, and announced that it would be glad to quote special rates "for camels, goats, horses, sheep and cattle."

Through the courtesy of the American Minister to Libya I got a lift from Tripoli to Benghazi in a U.S. military 'plane. We reached the field at dusk and had to circle it for an interminable time, because Libyan boys had to put out flares to mark the landing strip—paraffin torches which they lit by hand. There were no other lights available.

Benghazi is a miserable city, one of the most miserable I saw in all Africa. It was half destroyed by bombing during the Second World War, and ten years after the war gangs of workmen were still shovelling up debris. Disposal of wartime scrap, in fact, was a big and profitable business here. People lived on their own ruins—literally.

Benghazi seems to be a million miles from Tripoli, although the flight takes only three hours. But here we are in Africa, not Europe, and a slatternly Africa at that. Bedouins and their camels pitch camp just off the main streets.

The population is about sixty thousand, of whom perhaps twenty thousand are literate. The circulation of the local newspaper is six thousand, which is quite good for Libya.

The Arabs here are much stricter than those in Tripoli, and are more inclined to wear native dress. Of course they never, under any circumstances, bring their wives to a public—or private—function. If you want to make a sensation at a dinner party in Benghazi, ask any Arab guest if he thinks that women should be unveiled. He will be very indignant indeed.

Below Benghazi is the Sand Sea of Calanscio, which is probably the most difficult desert to penetrate on earth. Below this is Kufra, once famous as the "lost oasis." It was never seen by a European until a German explorer got there in 1881, and has been seen by very few Europeans since. You can reach Kufra from Benghazi in ten days by jeep, or forty by camel, but you will not find much there. In twenty thousand square miles there are only 432 people!

To sum up: Libya's political and economic problems are still grave. If the country doesn't manage to remain united, and doesn't continue to receive foreign aid, it may very well collapse. But give it food, give it schooling, and it can develop. Its future—like the future of any child—depends on how well it is nourished and brought up.

So far Libya hasn't cost its parents very much. Certainly the cost of keeping the country going will be less than the cost of surrendering it to chaos or Communism—two dangers which always threaten lands of poverty and ignorance.

10

Summing It Up

So we conclude our brief trip "meeting" the four countries of contemporary North Africa, with their lively assortment of peoples and problems. We have travelled a long way in space—from the wall of the Atlantic to the gates of Cairo near the Nile, and southward from the shores of the Mediterranean to the remote wastes of the Sahara. And we have travelled a long way in time, too—from the Phoenicians who built Carthage and their Berber predecessors who roamed over North Africa several thousand years ago all the way up to 1956, when Morocco and Tunisia, the newest countries in the world, joined the United Nations as independent sovereign states.

To sum up—Morocco is from some points of view almost like a Shangri-La—beautiful, remote and inexpressibly primitive. Here, in the fastnesses of the Atlas Mountains and in the craggy desert beyond, people have changed their way of life very little in the past centuries. The stern old rules of Islam still hold the people, untouched and undefiled. But in the towns, and indeed everywhere in the country except in the distant areas, a vast fermentation is going on. Morocco is being reborn. It is trying to become a modern state, against great difficulties, overnight. Morocco symbolizes the dramatic entrance of ancient, feudal Africa into the modern world.

Tunisia is also a symbol of this—even more so. This rugged little country typifies the struggle that is going on almost everywhere in Africa and Asia— the emergence of countries that have been controlled by European powers to a life of their own; in other words, their progress from colonialism to independence. How this evolution works out is, of course, a matter of great importance to all of us.

In Algeria a fierce struggle is going on between the French and the Arab rebels, and it is too early to tell what the final outcome will be. But Algeria has much of interest besides political tension and a tragic civil war. This country is an open doorway to the majesty and mystery of the Sahara, the greatest desert in the world. Even the Sahara is full of contrasts these days—the kind of contrasts that are so notable everywhere in North Africa. In the Sahara the Tuareg tribesmen, with their gaunt camels, stand cheek by jowl with European oil drillers with the most modern machinery. Africa is the place where the old and the new jostle each other all the time—where yesterday meets today.

Libya is mostly a "box of sand," but even sand can be interesting if only because there may be a lot of wealth underneath. The Libyans are striving hard and well to make their new country work; and it is very much to the general interest to see that it works well.

This is a wonderful part of the world we have been "meeting." It is even more wonderful to visit, to meet face to face, not just in the pages of a book. Go to North Africa some day, and see its marvels for yourself.

Glossary

abd—Arabic word for servant; used in many names, as Abdel (or abd el) Krim.

baboosh—a sandal or slipper, often gaily coloured.

baraka—a mystical quality believed to be possessed by holy men, giving them the power to bless their fellowmen and sometimes to foretell the future.

Barbary—from Berber, name given to original inhabitants of North Africa; Barbary Coast was the name Europeans formerly applied to the coast of North Africa, and pirates of this region were called Barbary pirates.

Bedouin—from an Arabic word meaning "desert dweller," used for certain nomadic Arab tribes.

Berber—from the Latin word meaning "foreigner"; name used by Romans for original inhabitants of North Africa.

bey—a Turkish title meaning "ruler"; also, until recently, the title of the ruler of Tunisia.

burnoose—hooded cloak sometimes worn over *djellaba*.

caid—a rural magistrate, or leader of a tribe.

caliph—literally a "successor"; title used for head of Moslems, who is believed to be a successor to the Prophet Mohammed.

colon—French for "colonist"; used to refer to French settlers in North Africa.

chott—a shallow or completely dried-up saline lake.

couscous—basic Arabian dish made of semolina, a wheat cereal, piled into a mound containing also bits of meat, nuts, vegetables or other ingredients.

Destour—literally "constitution"; name of a political party in Tunisia.

dey—*see* bey.

diffa—an Arabian banquet, consisting of many courses.

djellaba—long gown with a hood; the basic Arab garment.

emir—Arabic title meaning "chieftain."

fez—a red tarboosh; formerly made exclusively in the city of Fez.

fondouk—native inn catering to men and animals of a caravan.

hadj—title which may be used by any Moslem who has made the pilgrimage to Mecca; a hadj is usually known by the green turban which also signifies that he has made the pilgrimage.

ibn—son; used in many names, as in the full name of the Prophet Mohammed: Abul Quasim Mohammed Ibn Abd Allah.

imam—leader of Moslem prayers.

Imazighen—literally "free men"; name used for themselves by the tribal inhabitants of North Africa, whom Europeans call Berbers.

inshallah—Arabic word meaning "if Allah wills it"; a word used frequently by Moslems.

Islam—literally "submission" (to the will of God); the religion of the Moslems; also the Moslem world.

Istiqlal—literally "independence"; name of principal political party of Morocco.

jebel—Arabic for "hill."

karwâne—a relay point, as for caravans; forms of this word appear in the name of an important Tunisian city, Kairouan, and a famous mosque in Fez, Morocco, called the Kairouyine Mosque.

kasbah—fort or castle; also used for the native quarter of a North African town.

Koran—the holy book of the Moslems.

Maghreb—name applied in ancient times to the greater part of North Africa; still occasionally used today.

marabout—a holy man; or his home or tomb which has become a shrine.

medina—native quarter of a North African city.

mehara—special highly prized breed of dromedary.

meharist—French or native mounted soldier using a mehara.

mellah—literally "salt"; used as name of Jewish quarter of North African city.

milrah—small niche, indicating direction of Mecca, in Moslem mosque.

minaret—the slender tower on a mosque.

minbar—short flight of stairs in a mosque, used as a pulpit.

Moslem—one who follows the teachings of the Prophet Mohammed and accepts him as the Messenger of the Moslem god, called Allah; Moslems do not like to be called Mohammedans.

mosque—(in Arabic *masjid*), literally "a place to bow down"; a building for public Moslem worship.

muezzin—man who calls faithful Moslems to their five daily prayers, speaking from minaret or door of mosque.

Neo-Destour—Tunisian political party; an offshoot of the Destour.

pasha—provincial governor or head of municipal administration; may thus be leader of large group of tribes.

piste—unpaved desert road.

Ramadan—a month of special prayers and fasting in the Islamic calendar.

Shiite—a Moslem sect; from the Arabic word for "party."

sidi—a title meaning roughly "His Excellency."

sook—a booth or market.

sultan—Turkish title given to Turkish governors of North African provinces; also, until recently, title of ruler of Morocco.

Sunna—a book of laws and regulations which, together with the Koran, form the basis of the Islamic tradition.

Sunnites—a Moslem sect: from Sunna.

tarboosh—brimless felt hat; a turban may be wrapped around it, so that only the top of the crown is left exposed.

Tuareg—a group of Berber desert dwellers; sometimes called the blue-veiled Tuareg because the men wear dark blue veils.

zakah—sum of money which all Moslems are expected to contribute to charity each year.

Index